Therapeutic Colouring book II

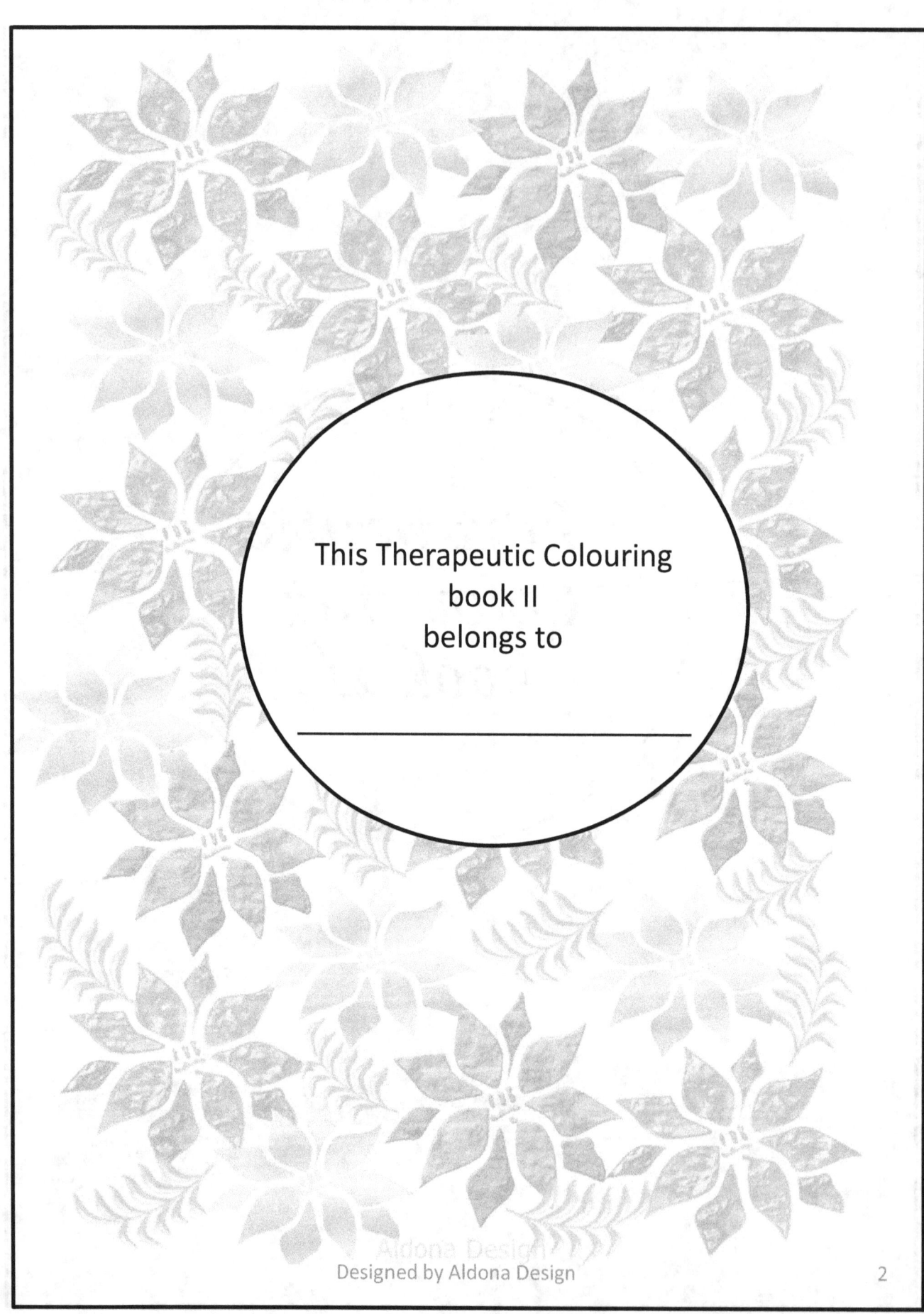

This Therapeutic Colouring
book II
belongs to

_____

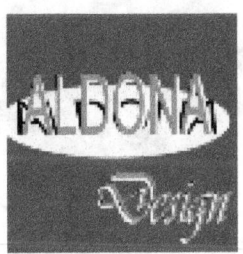

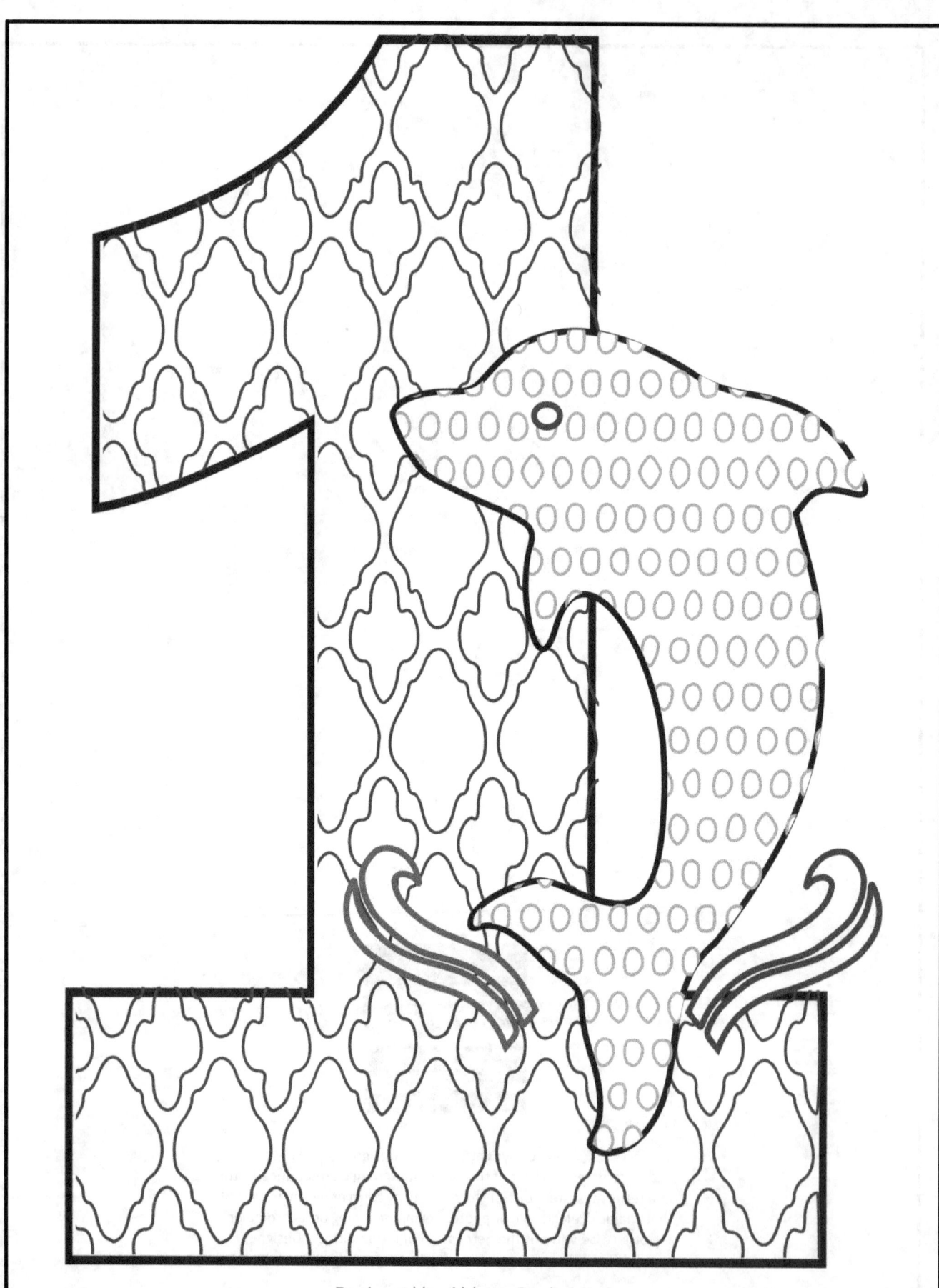

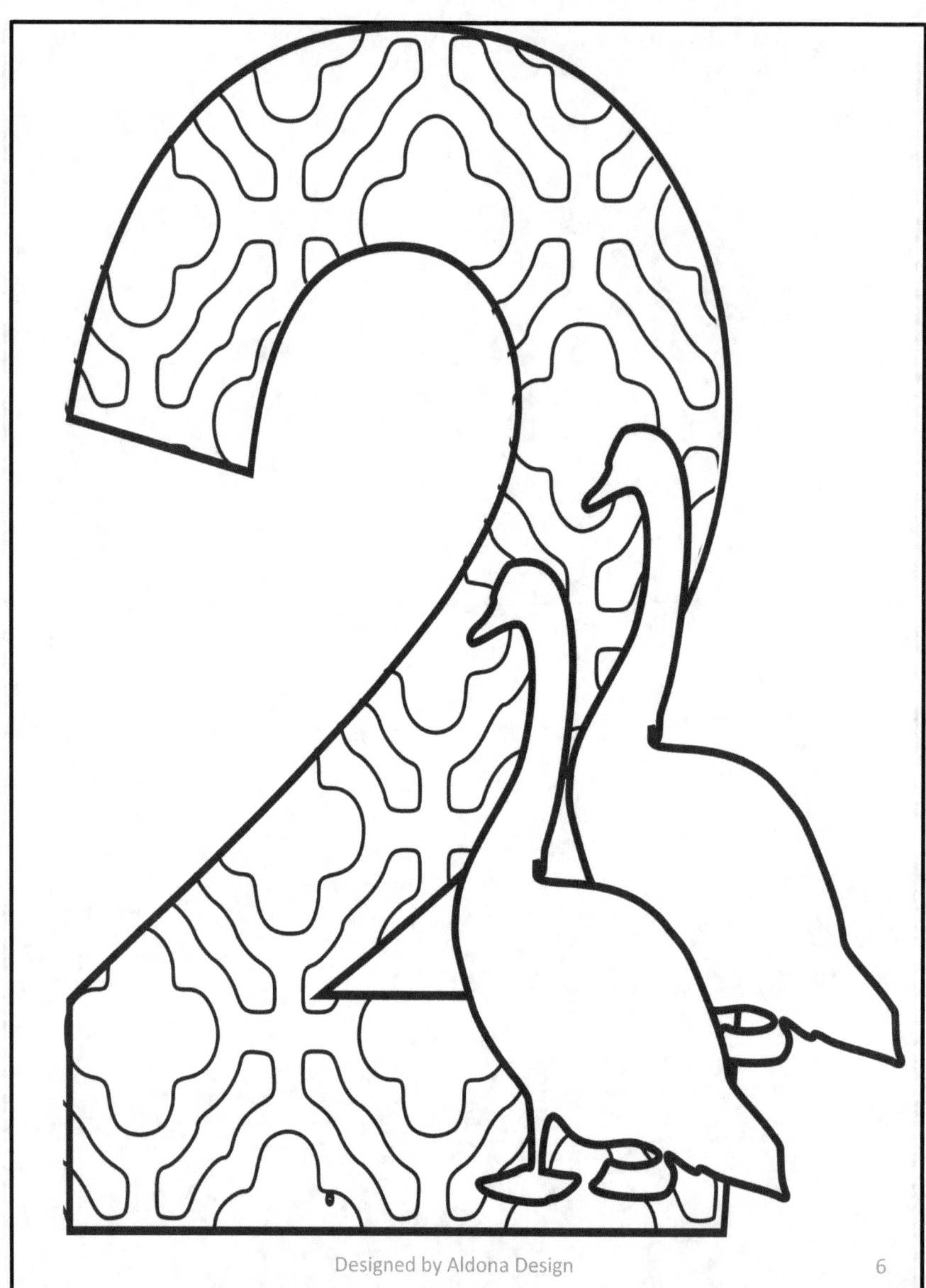

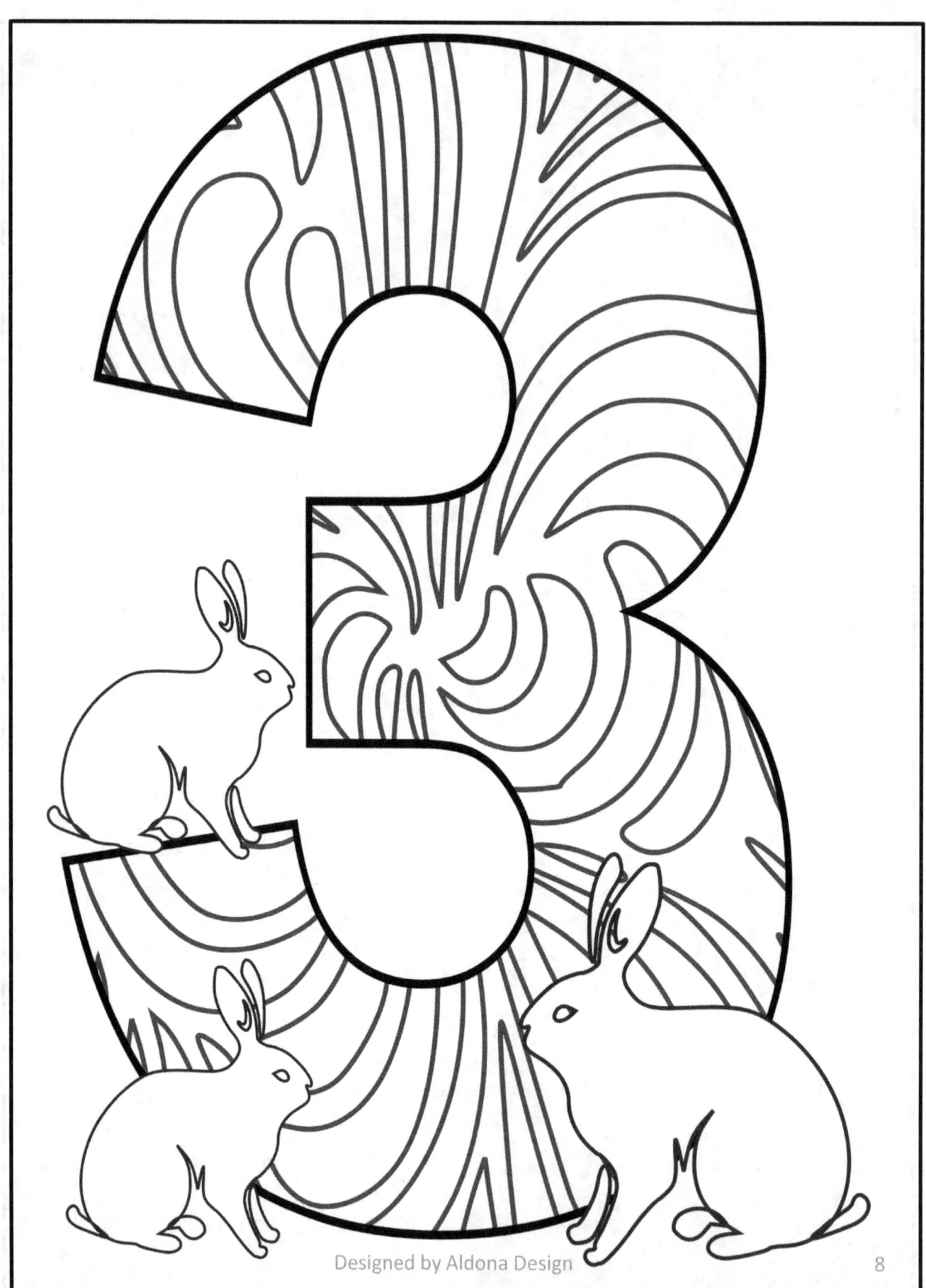

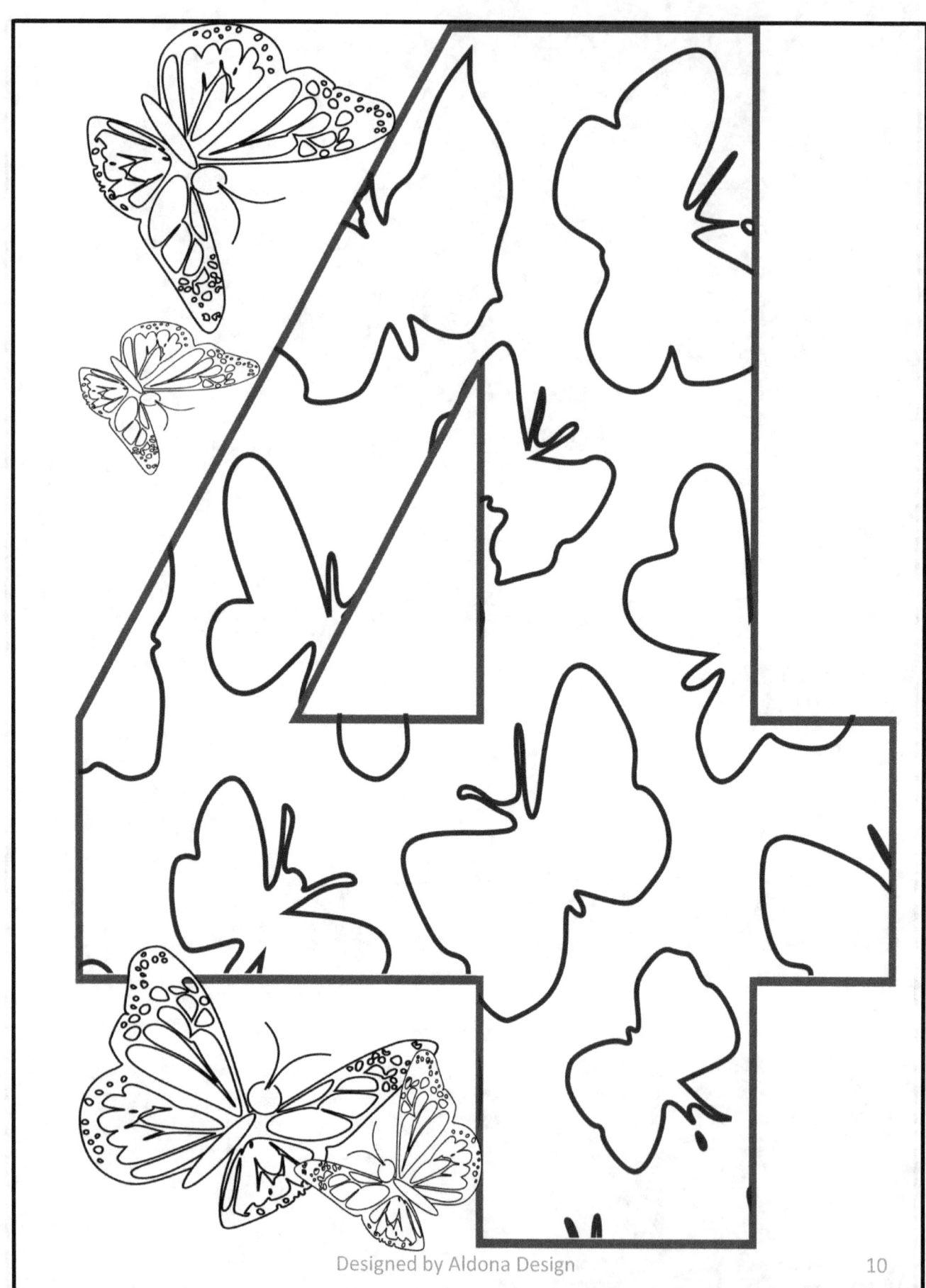

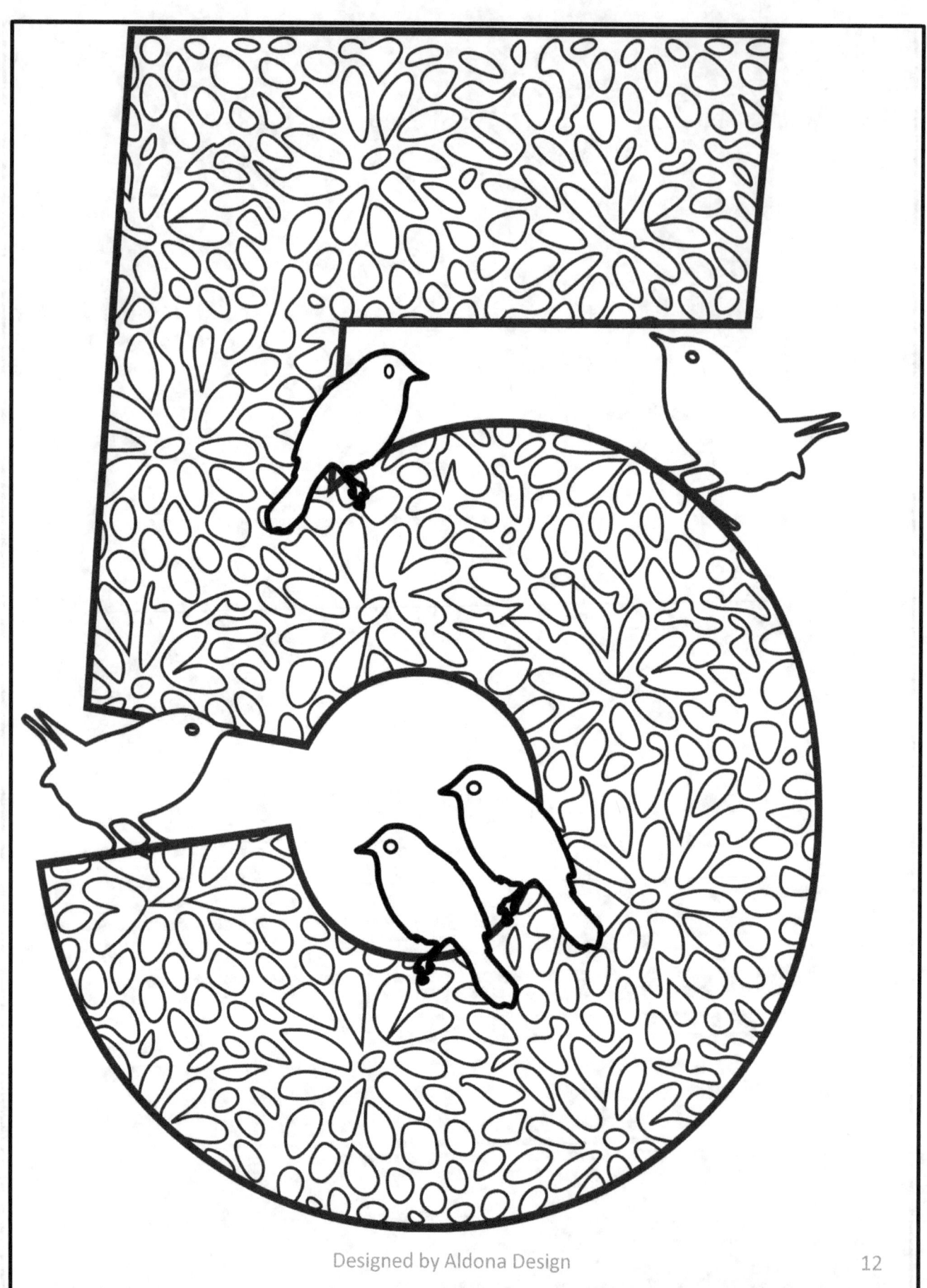

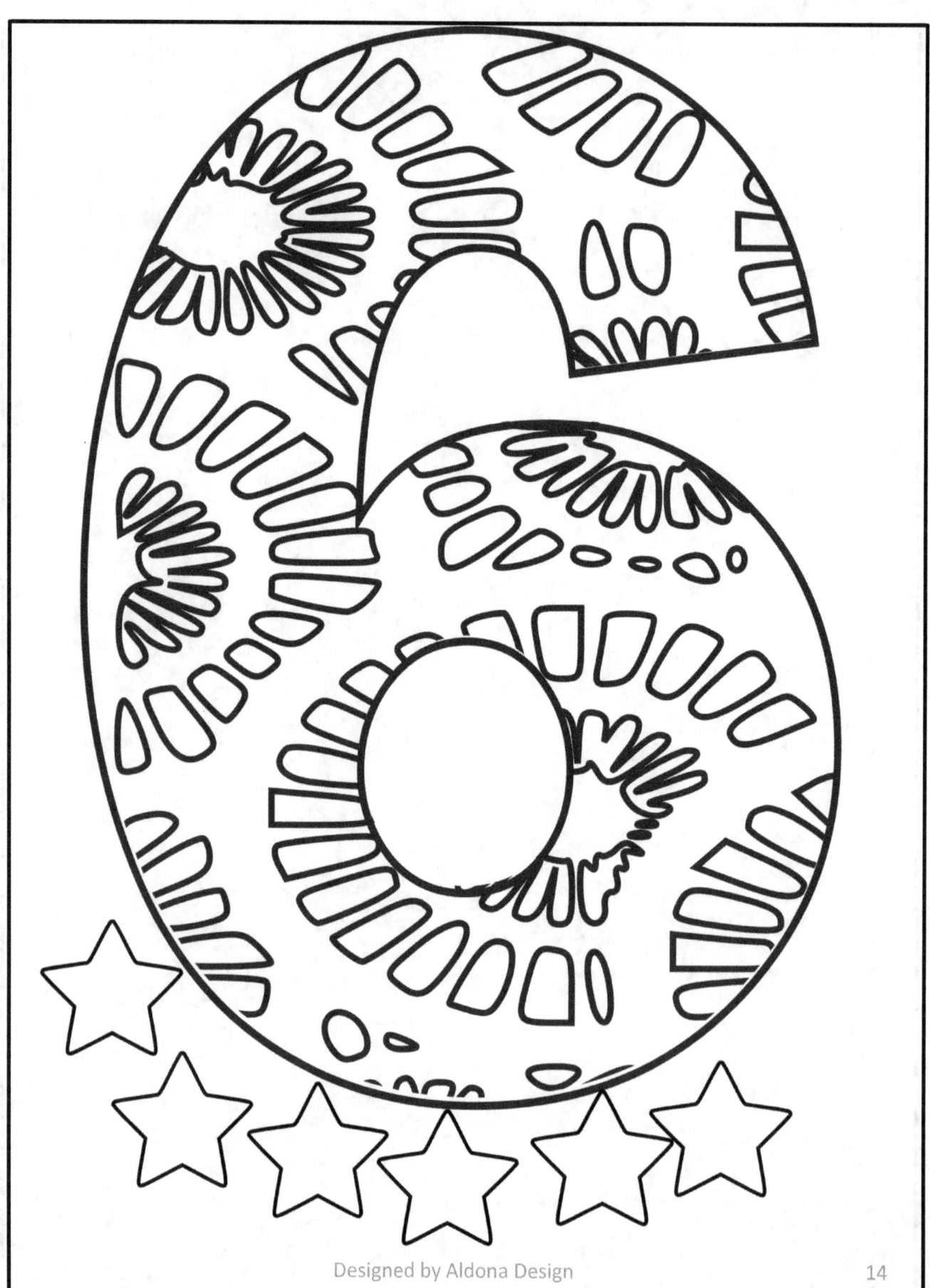

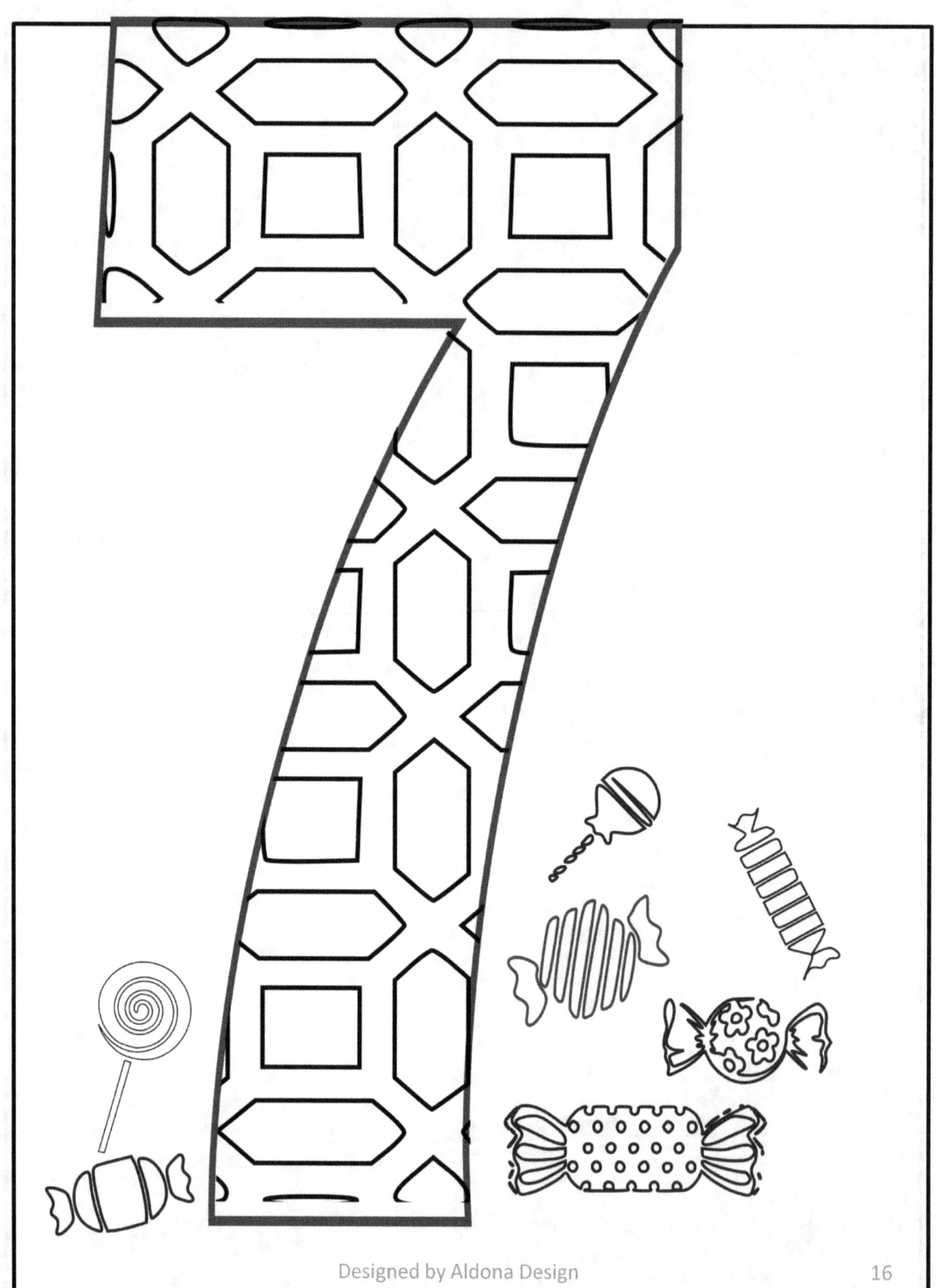

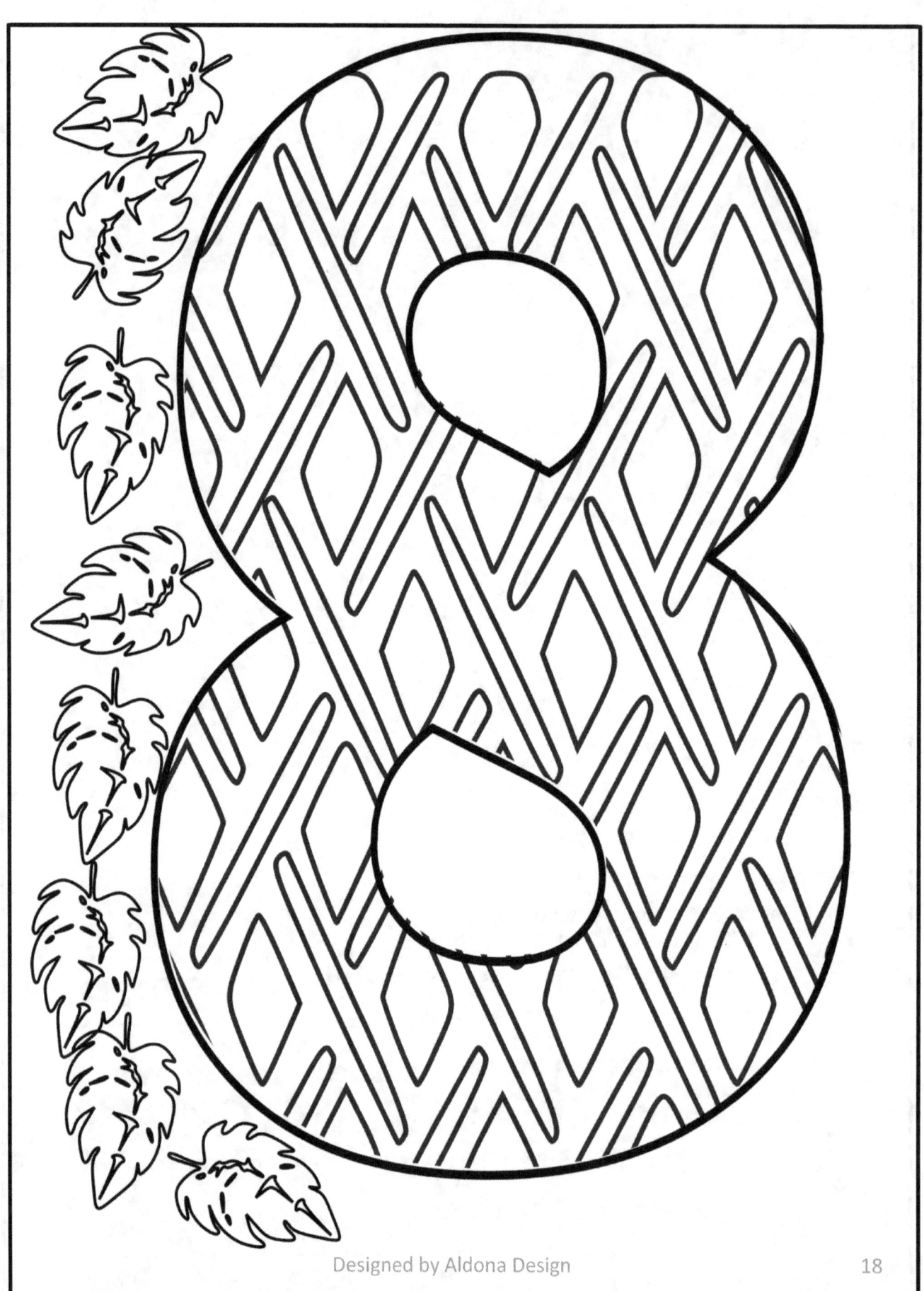

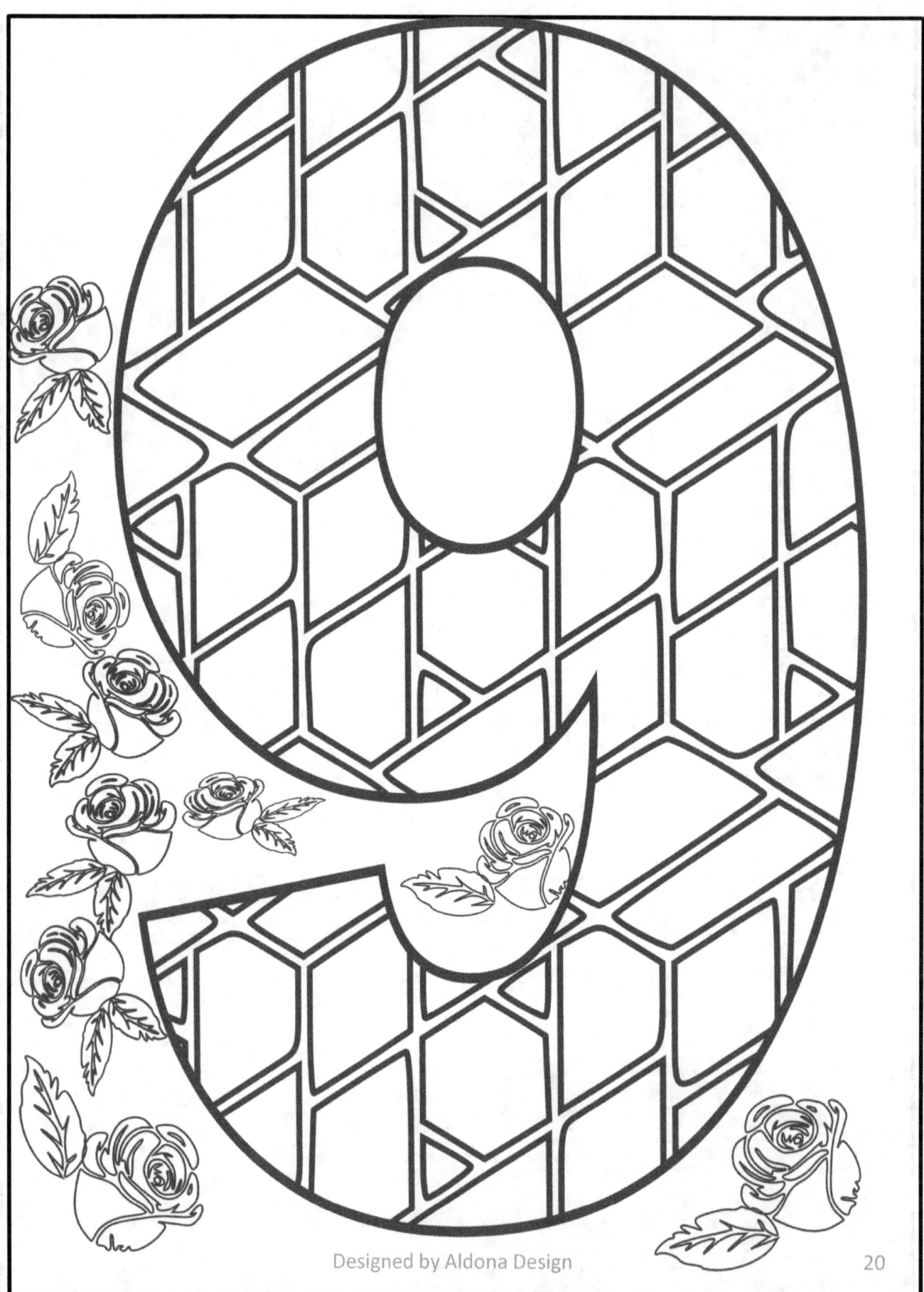

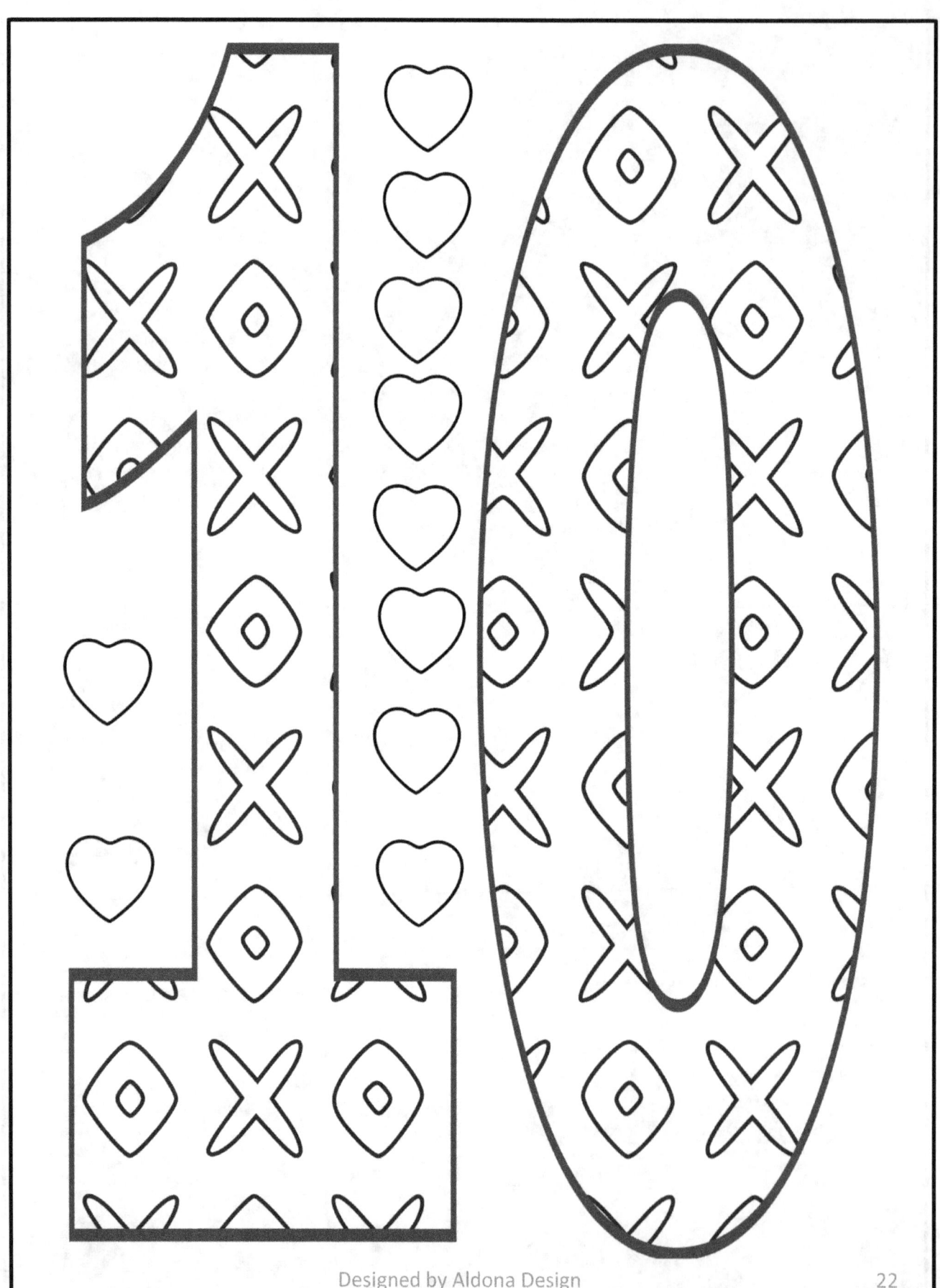

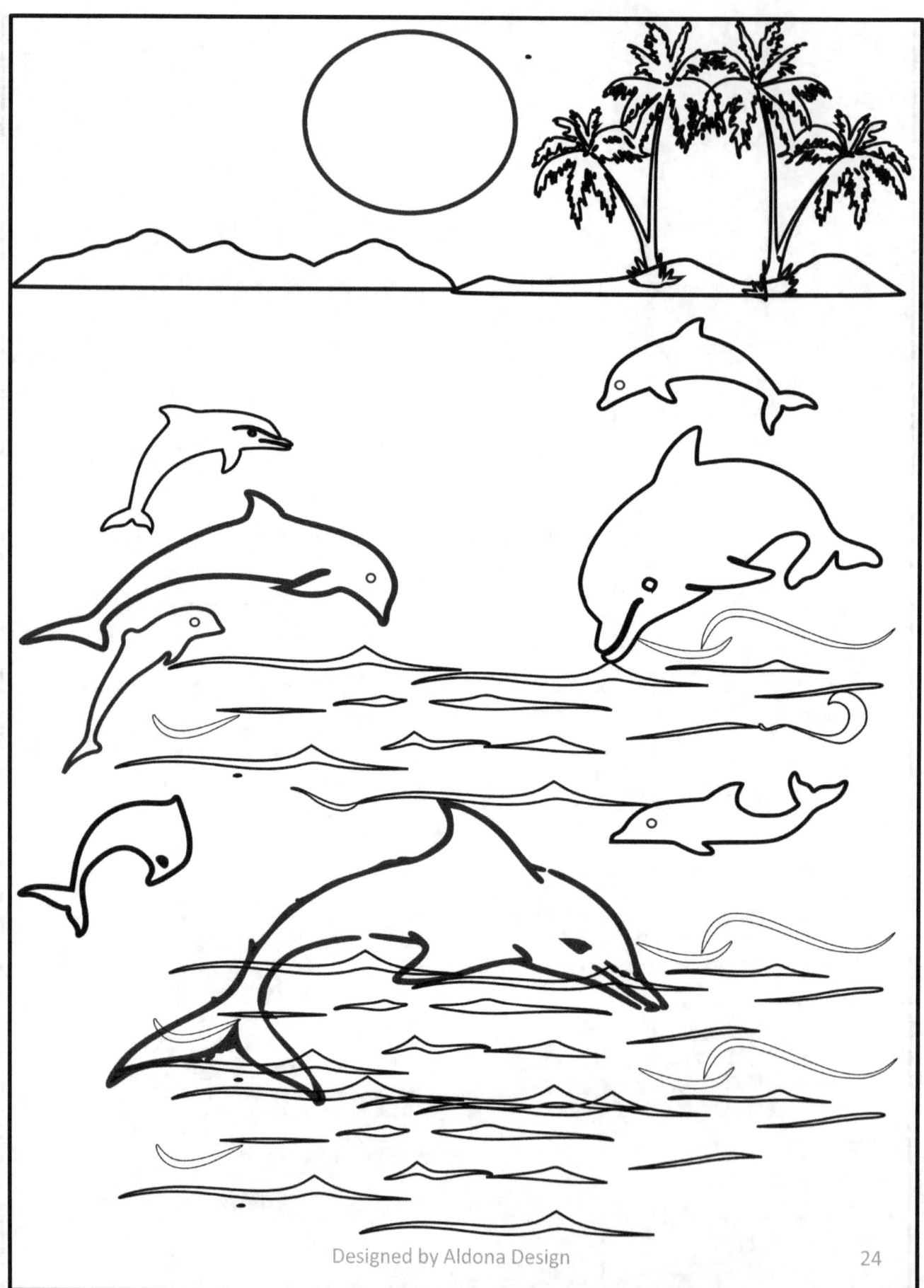

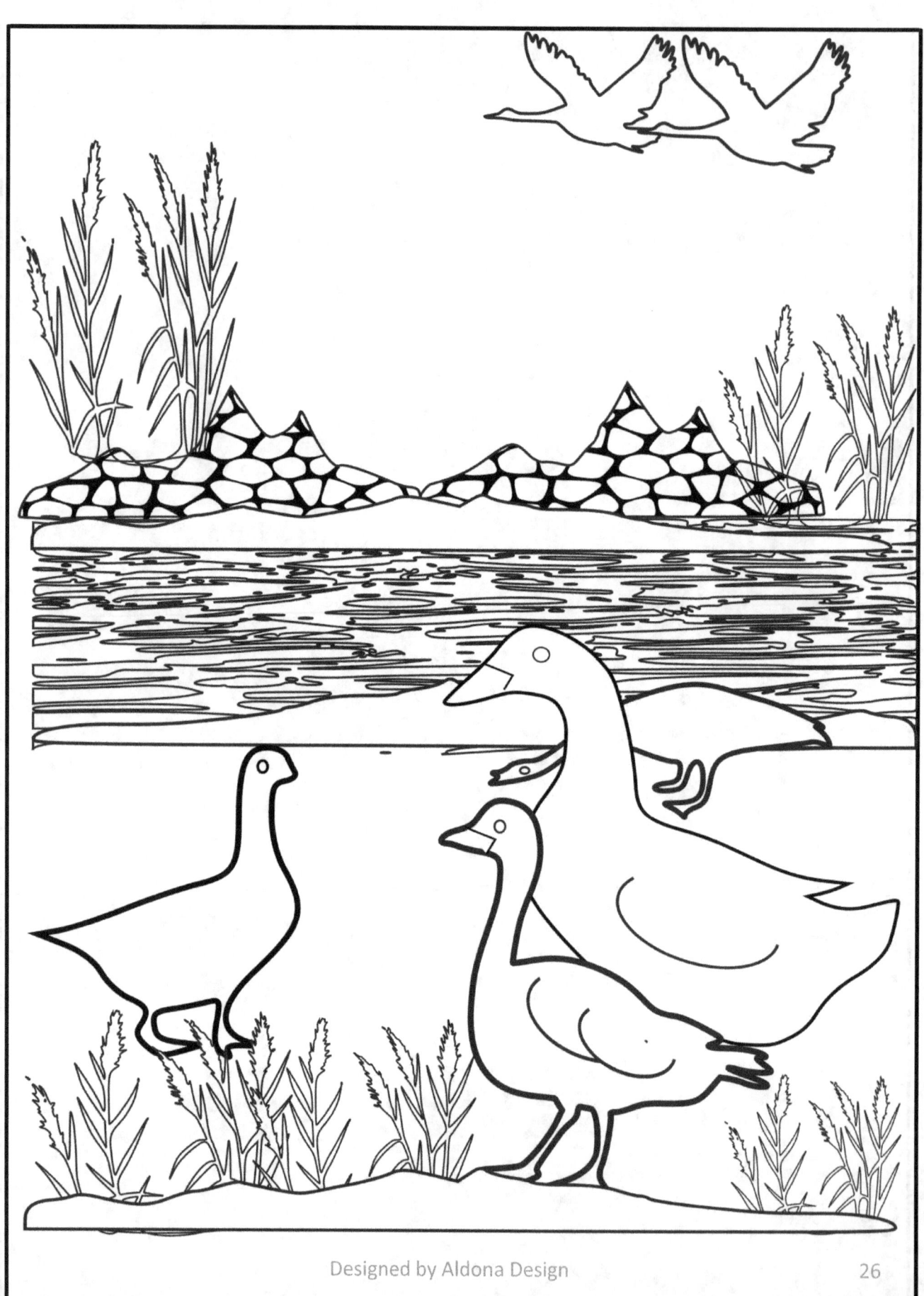

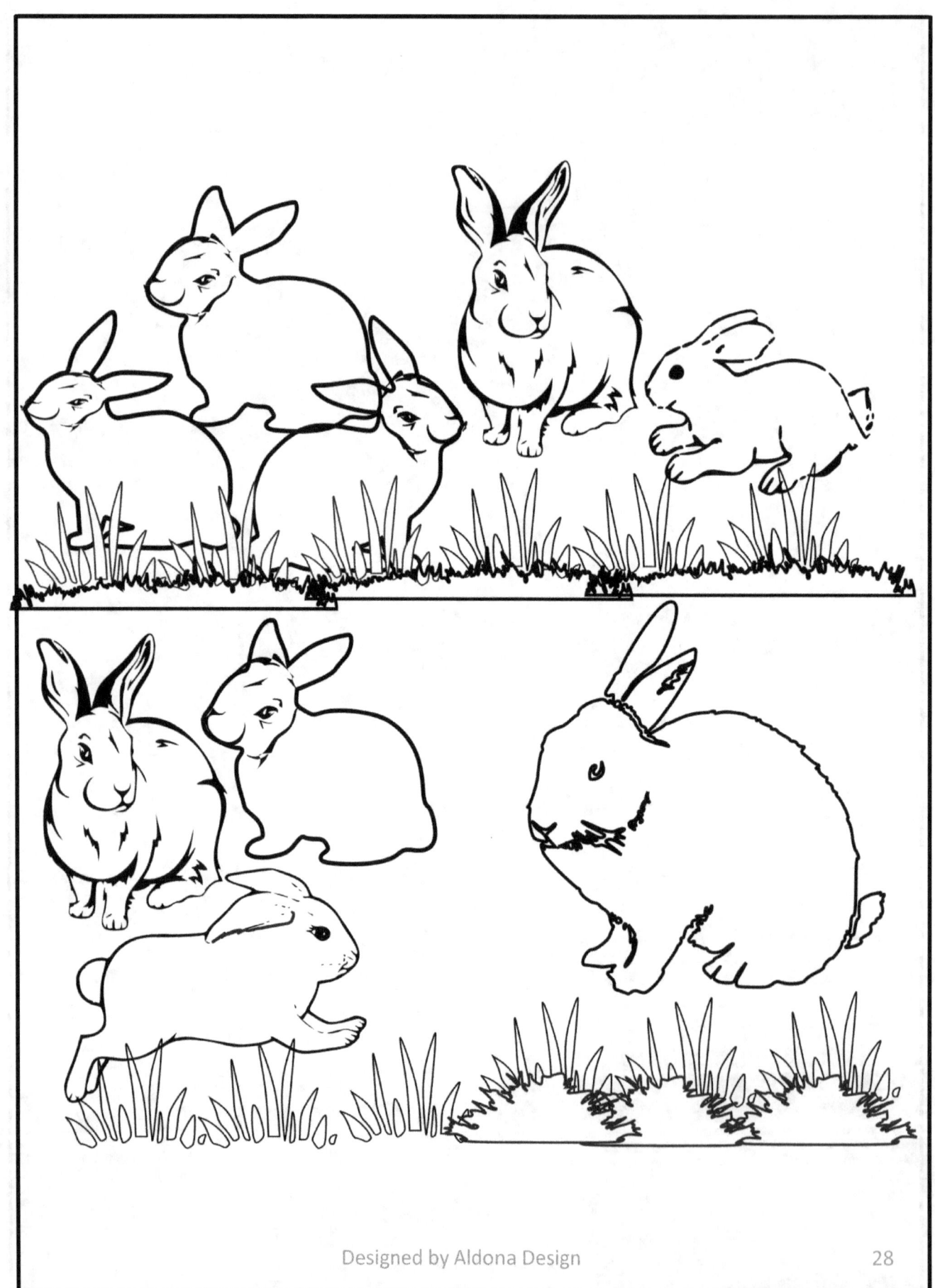

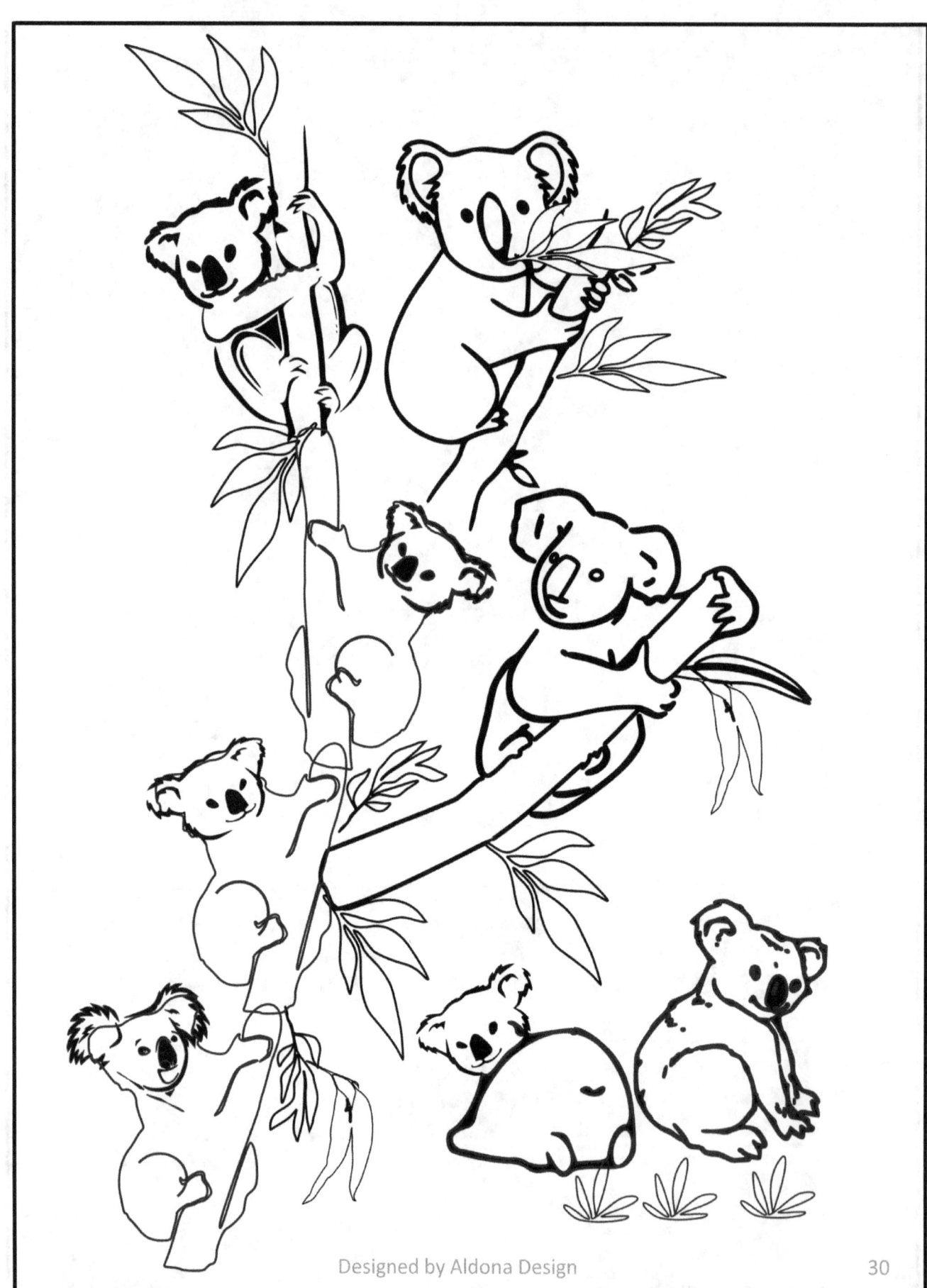

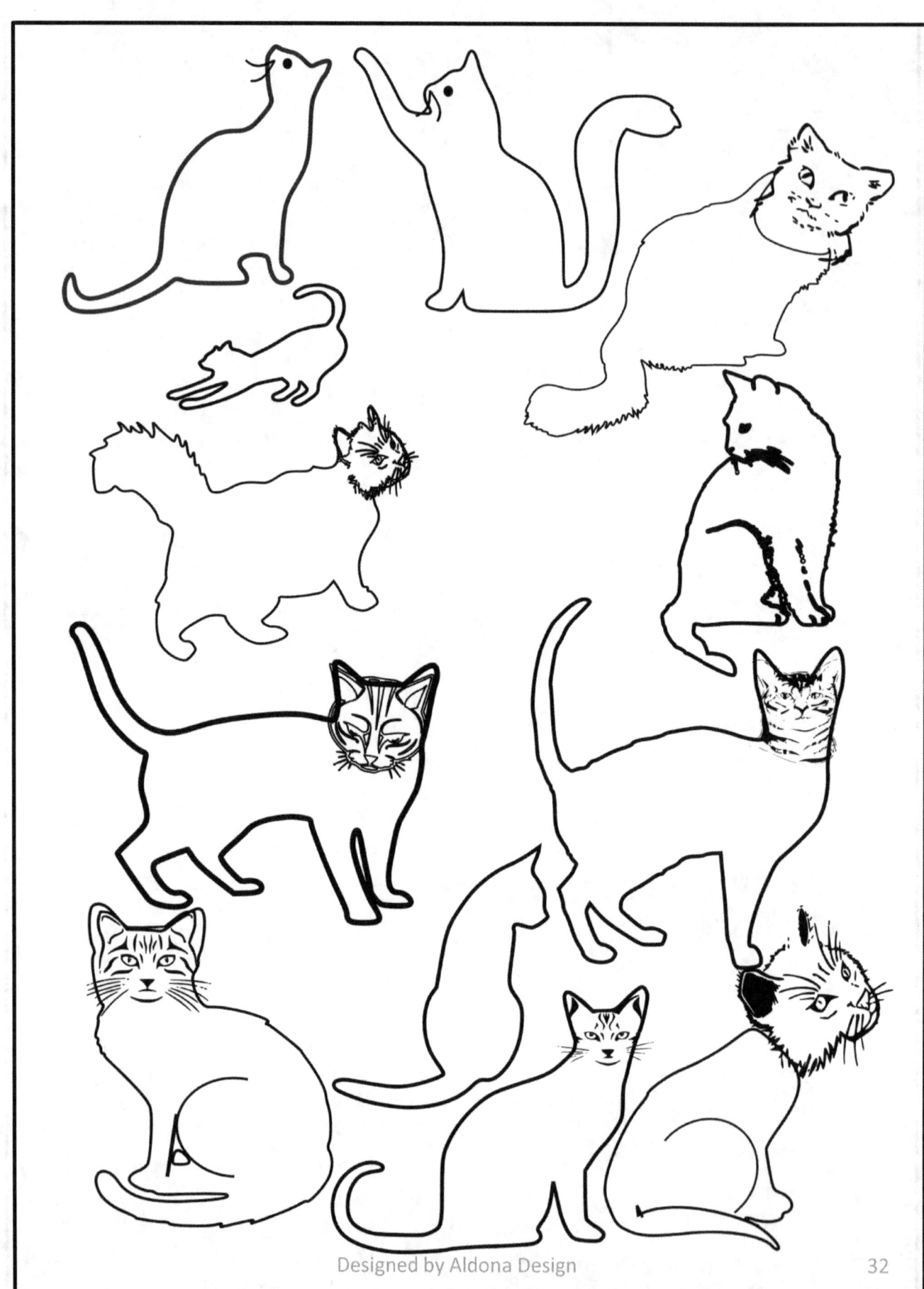

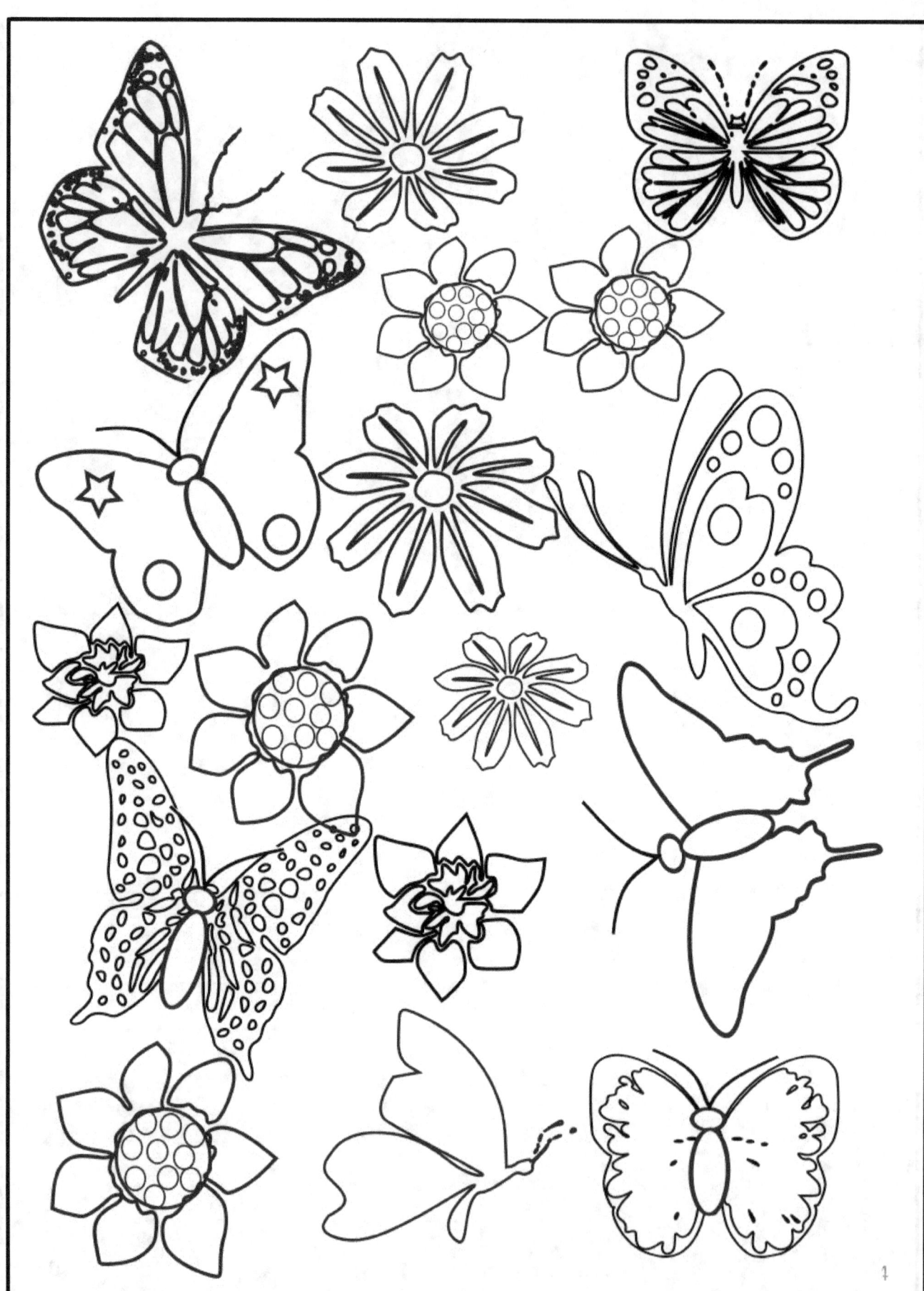

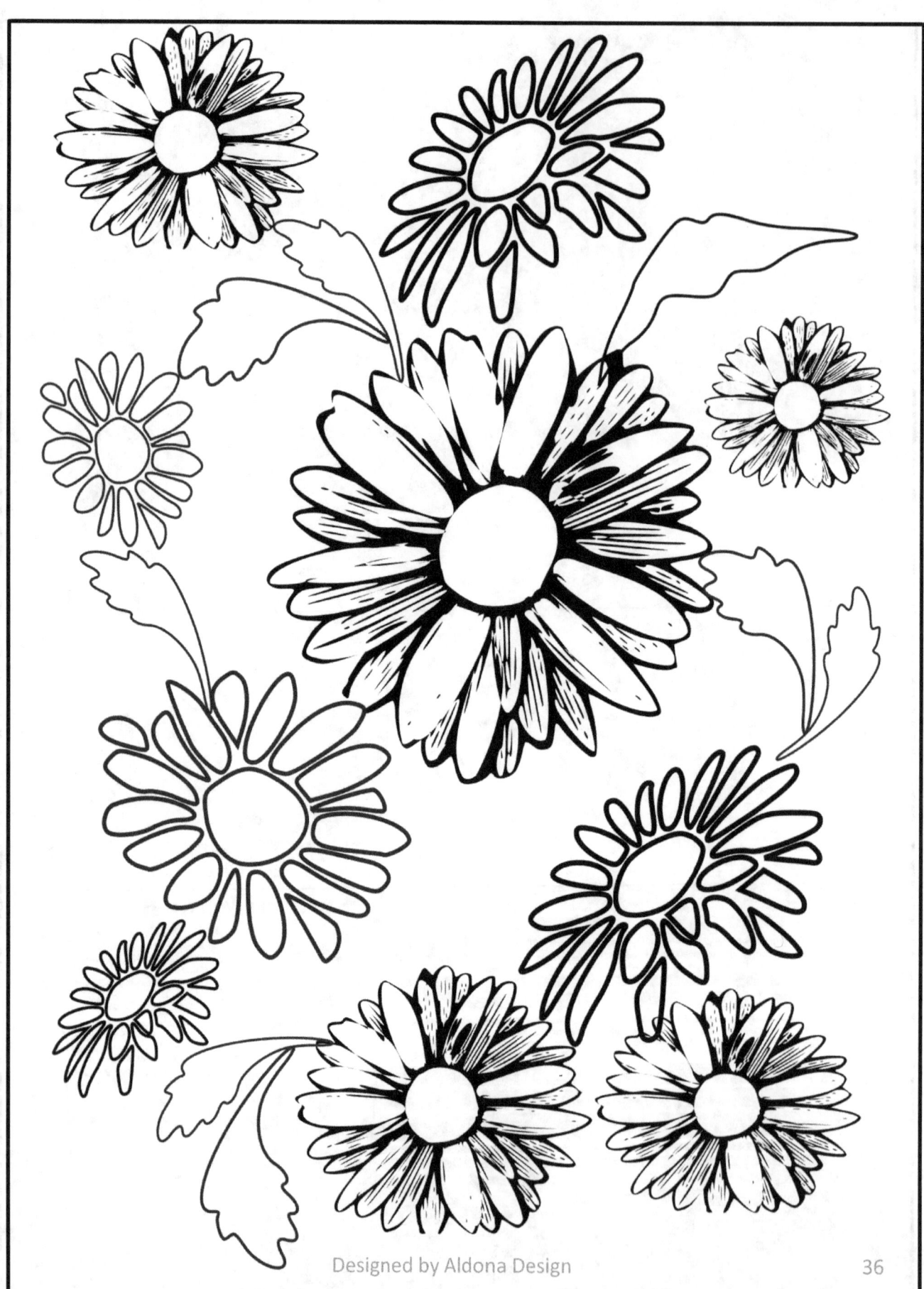

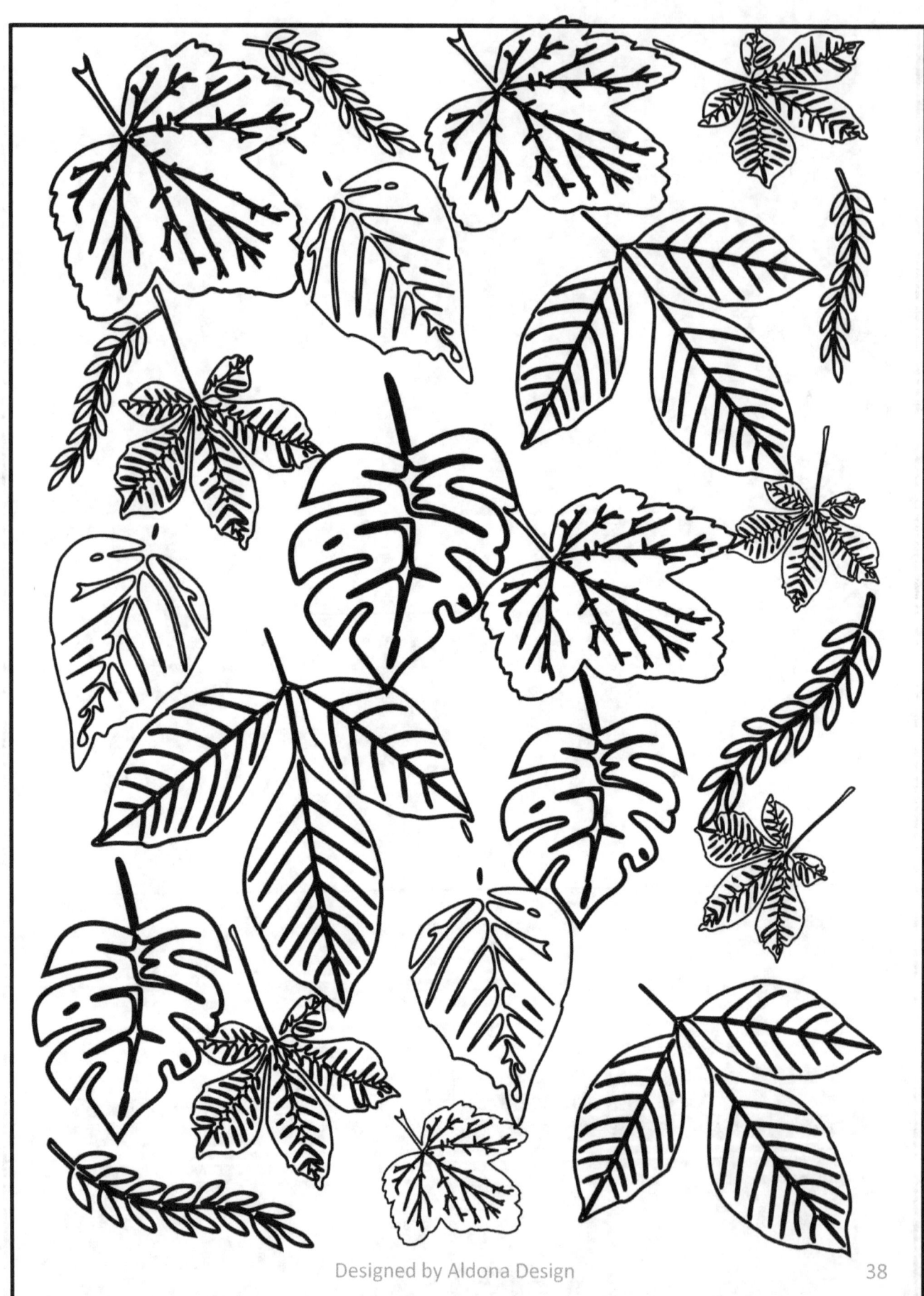

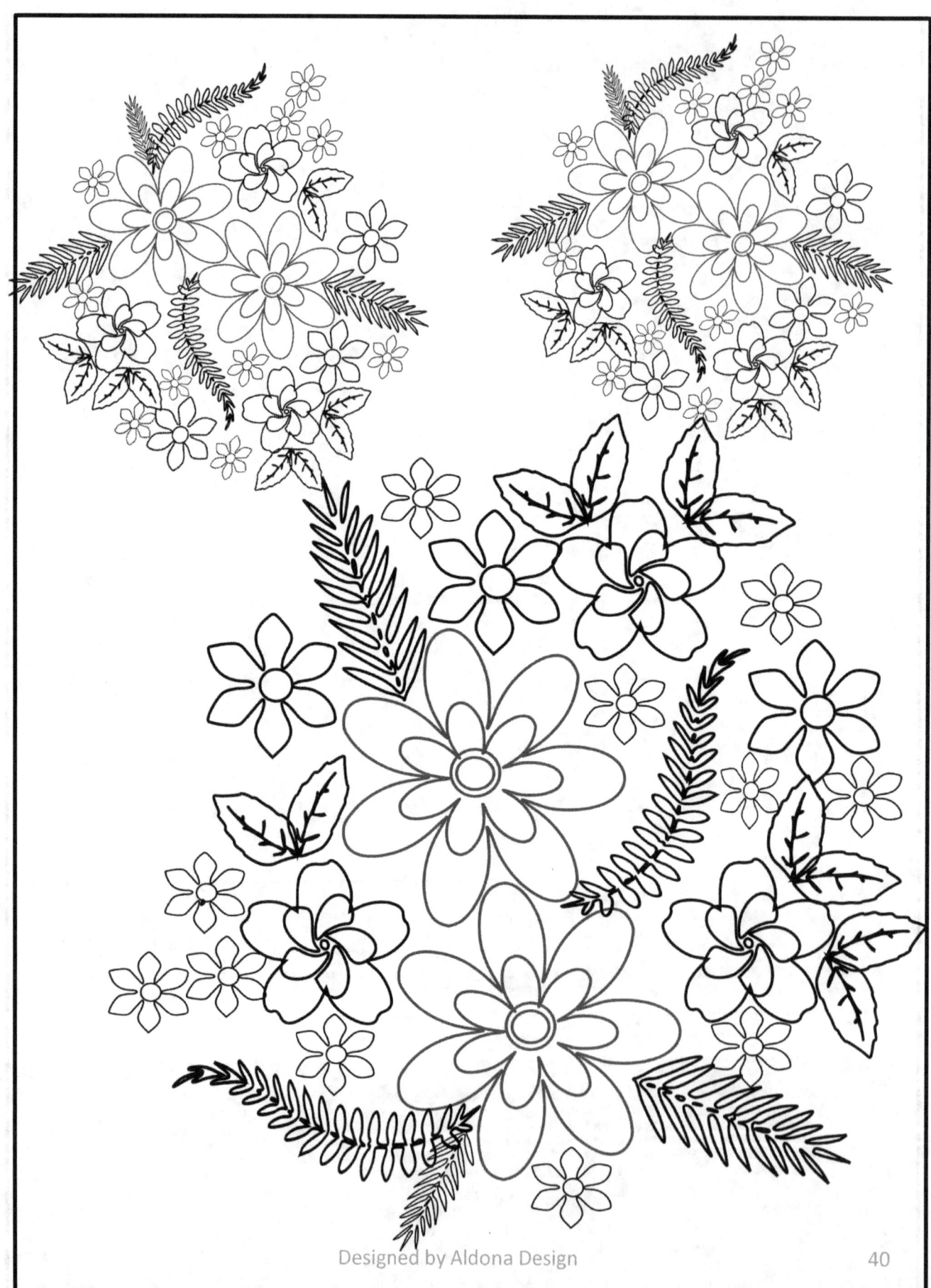

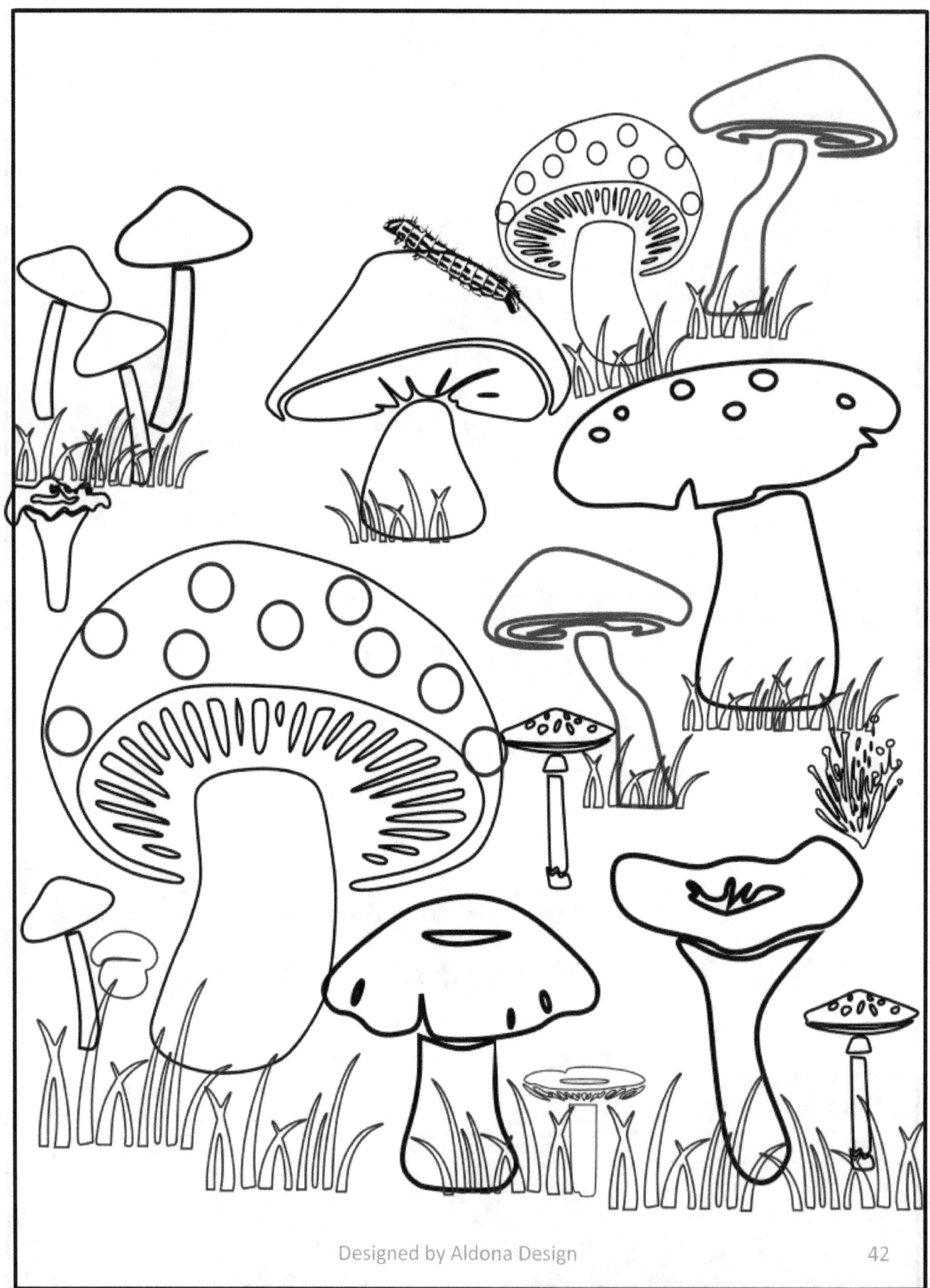

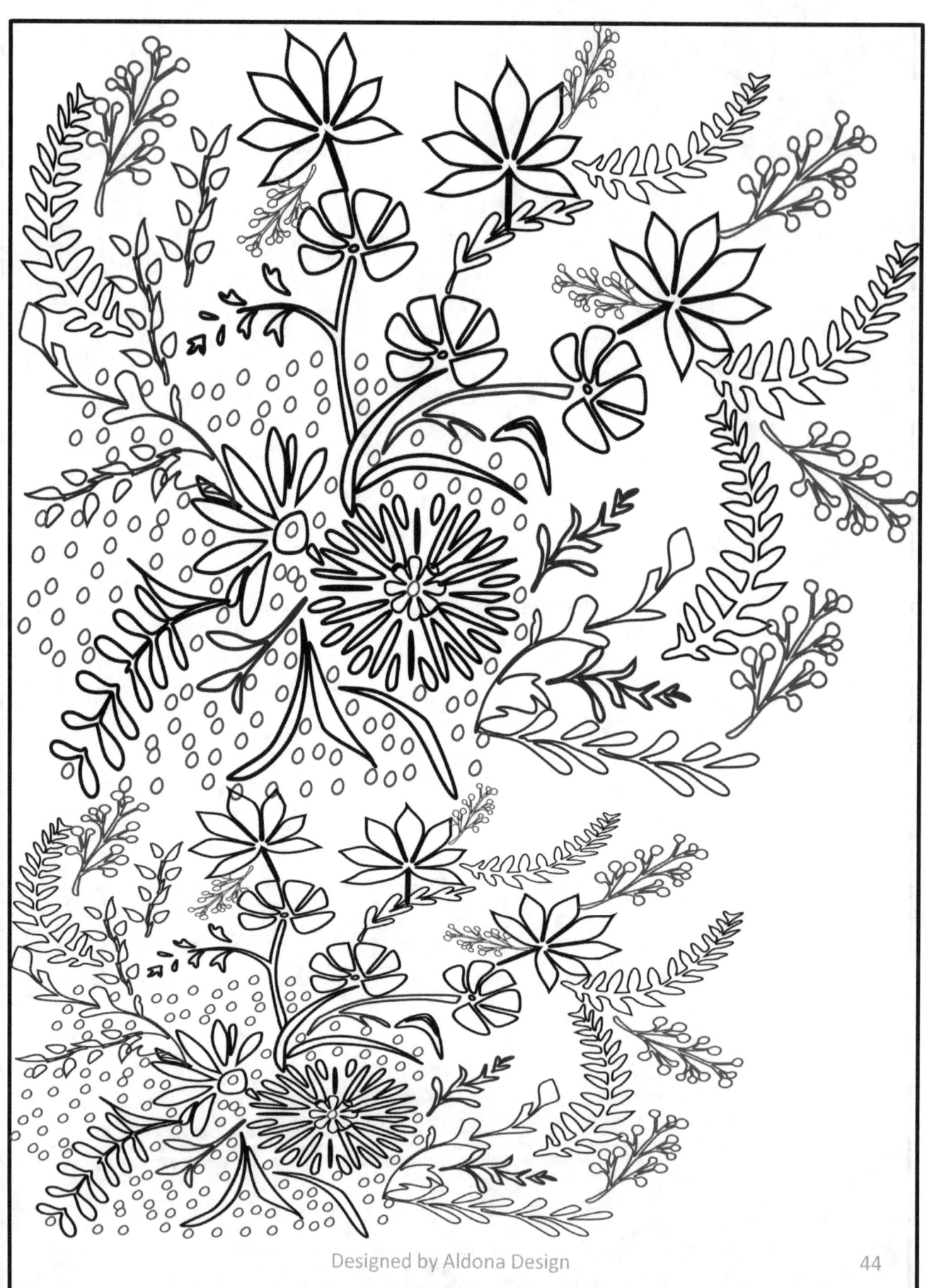

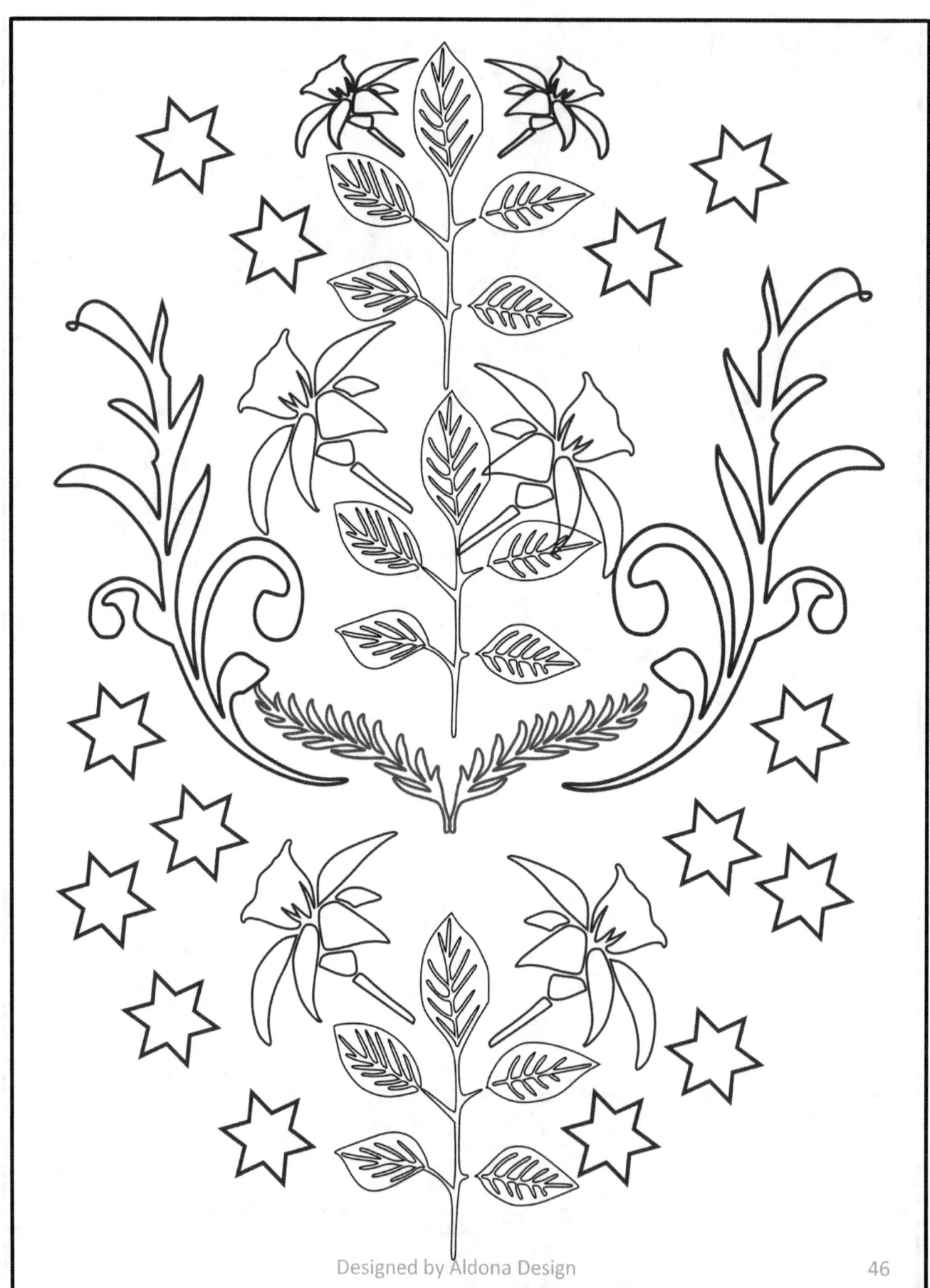

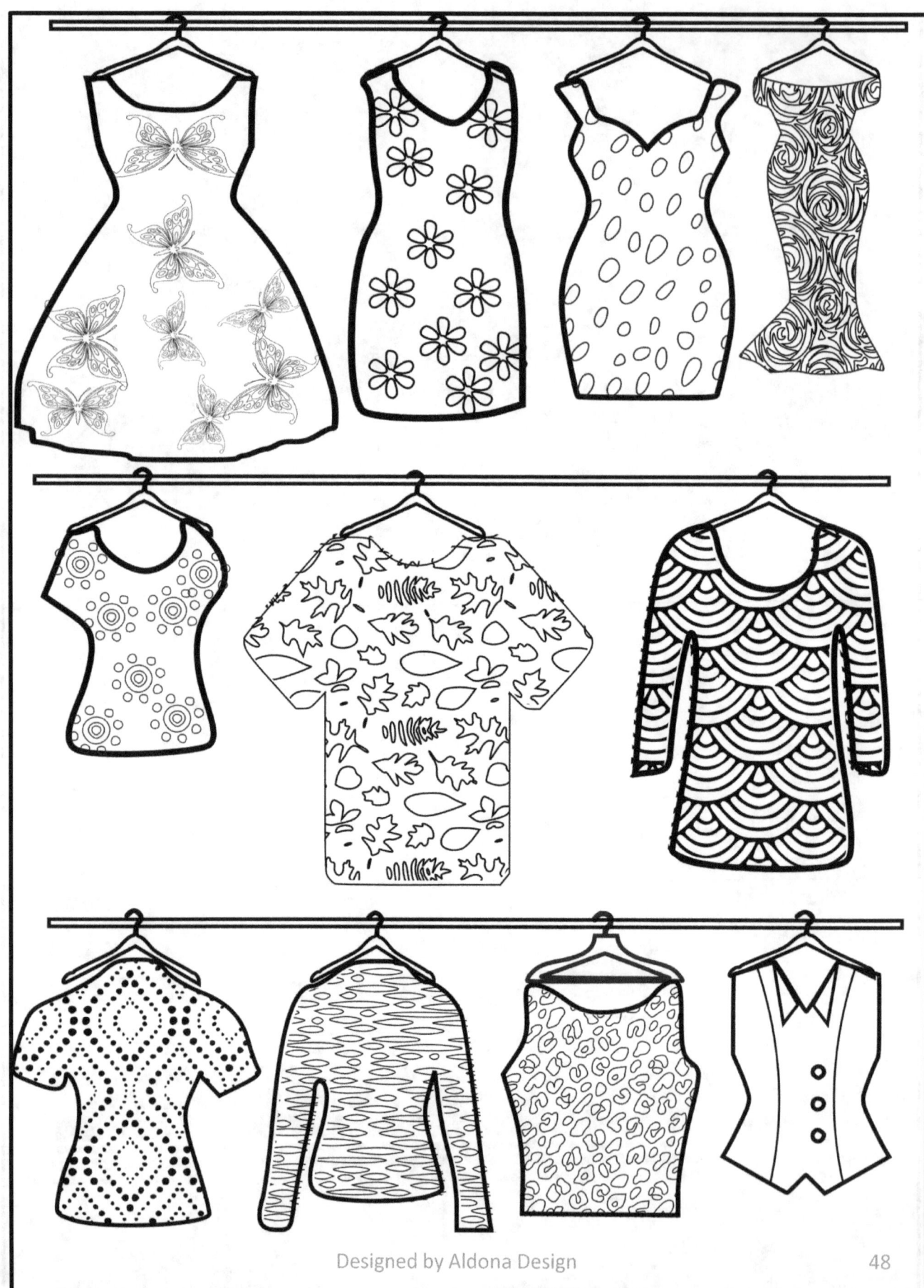

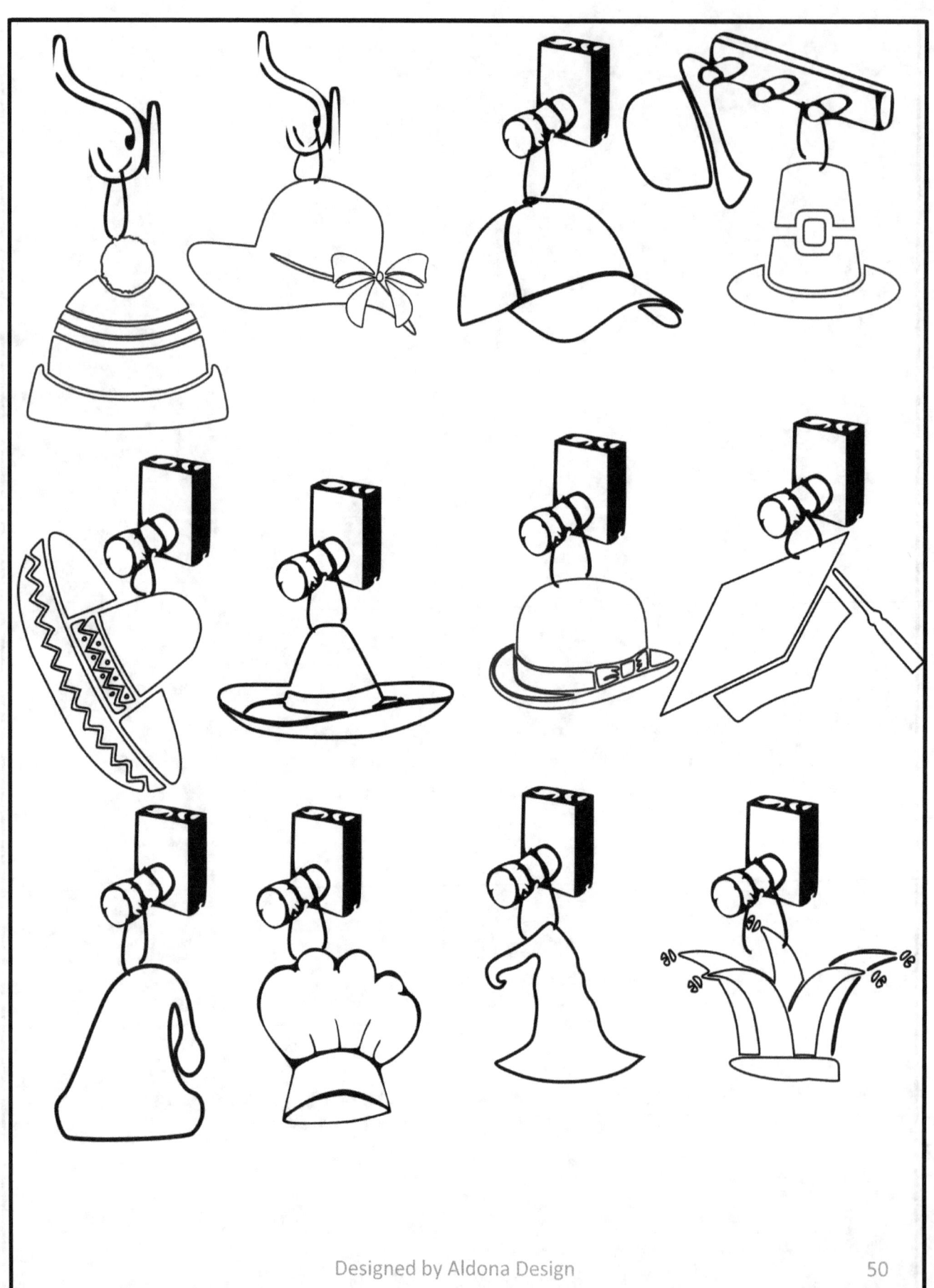

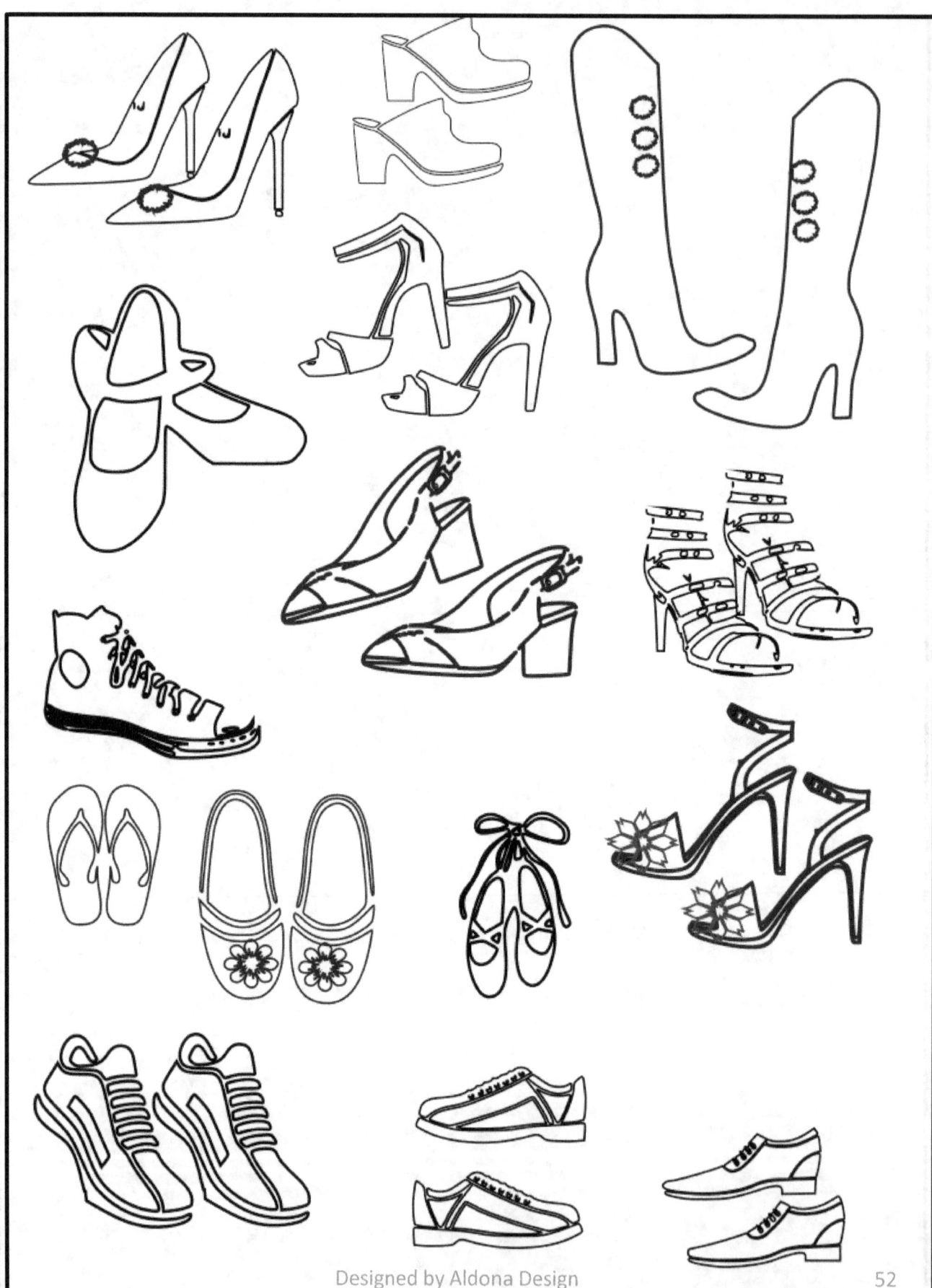

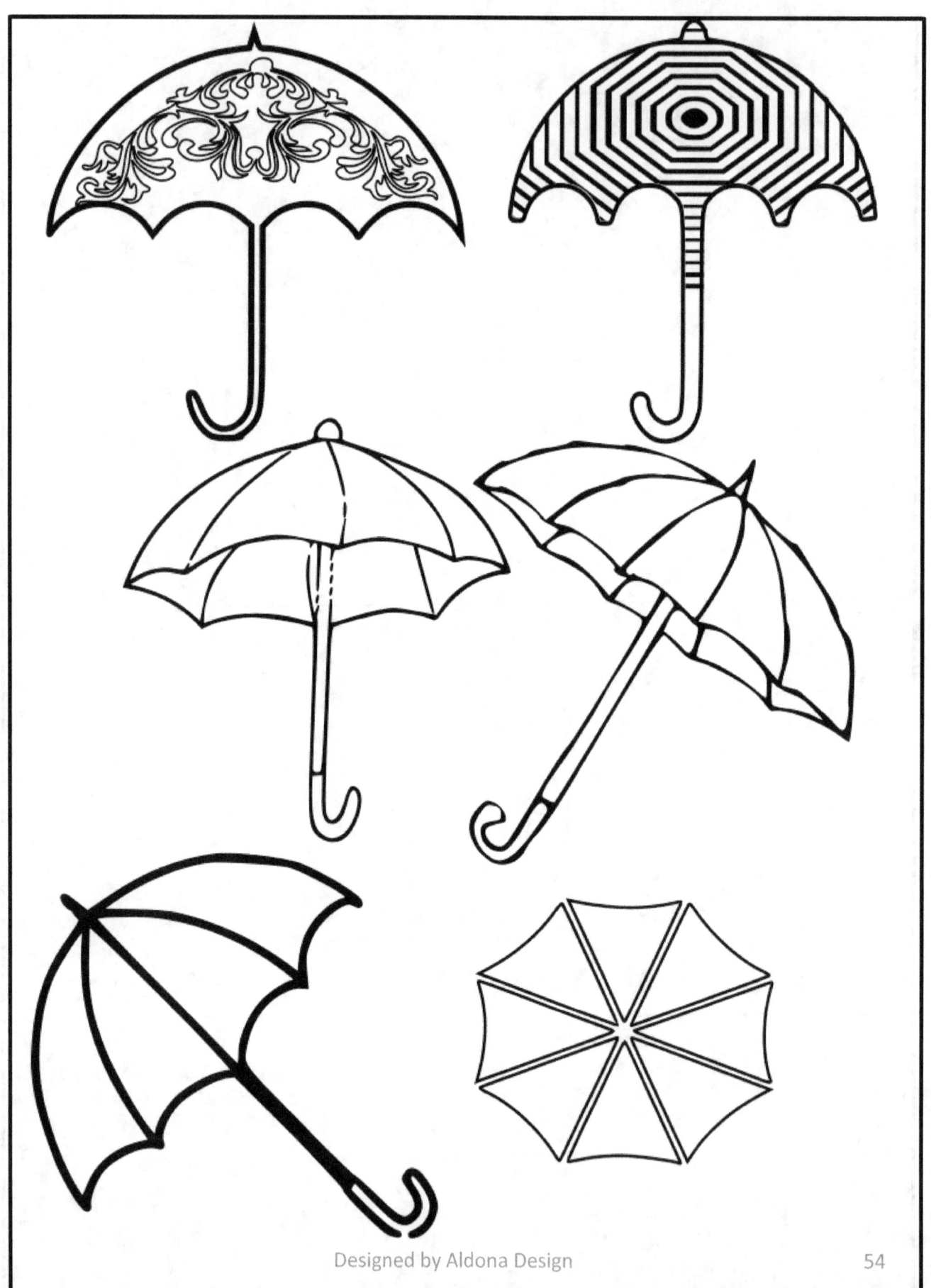

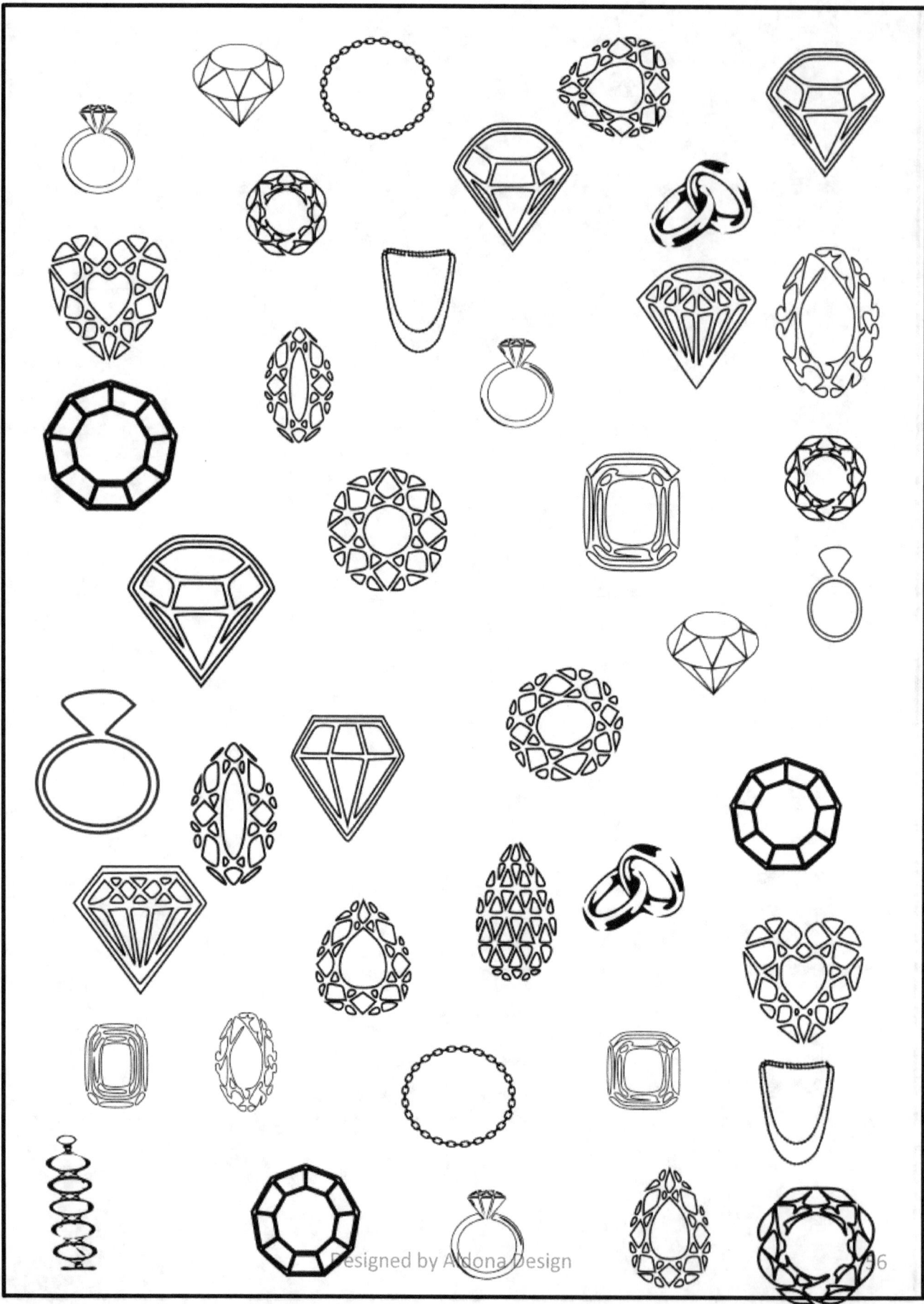

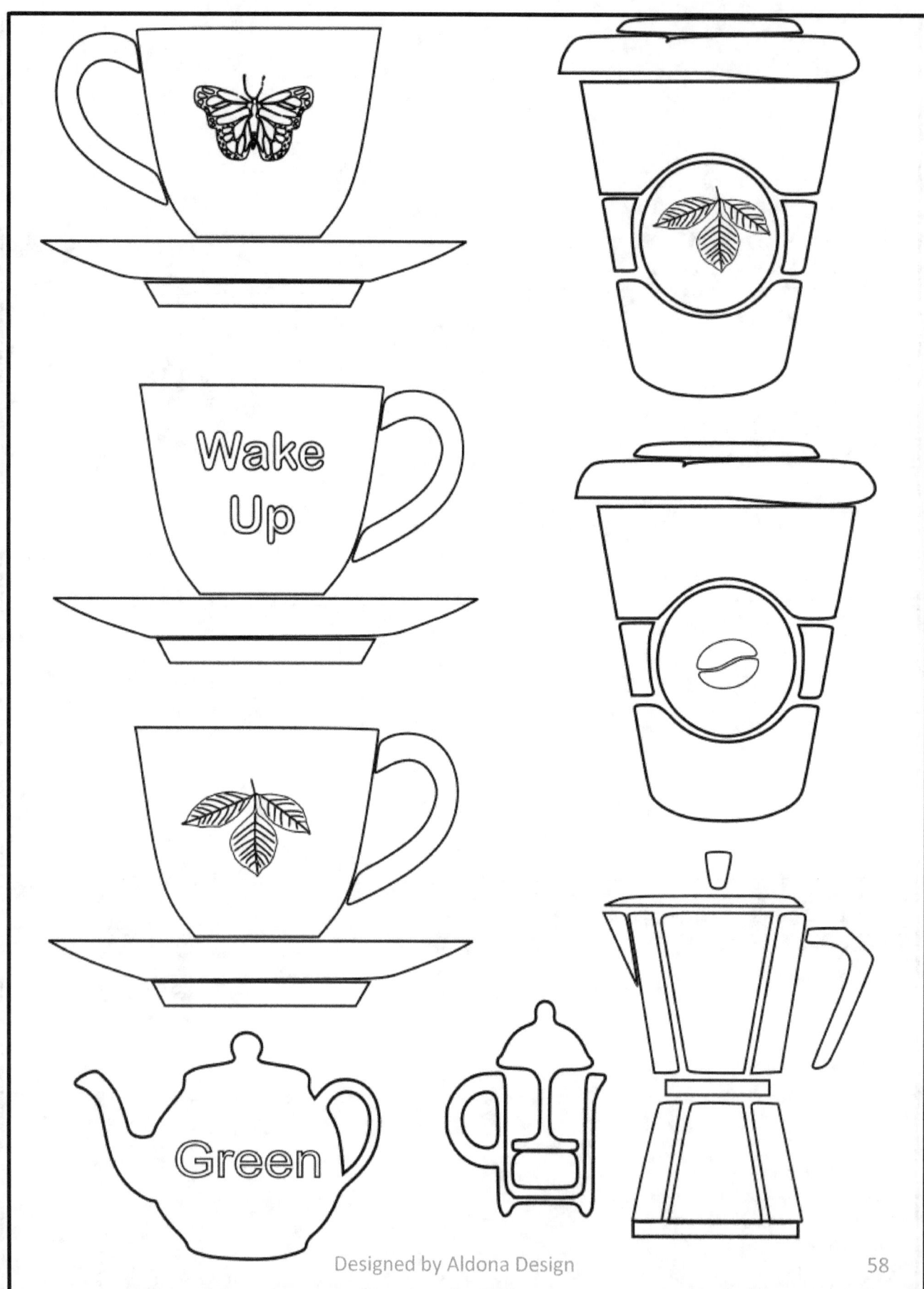

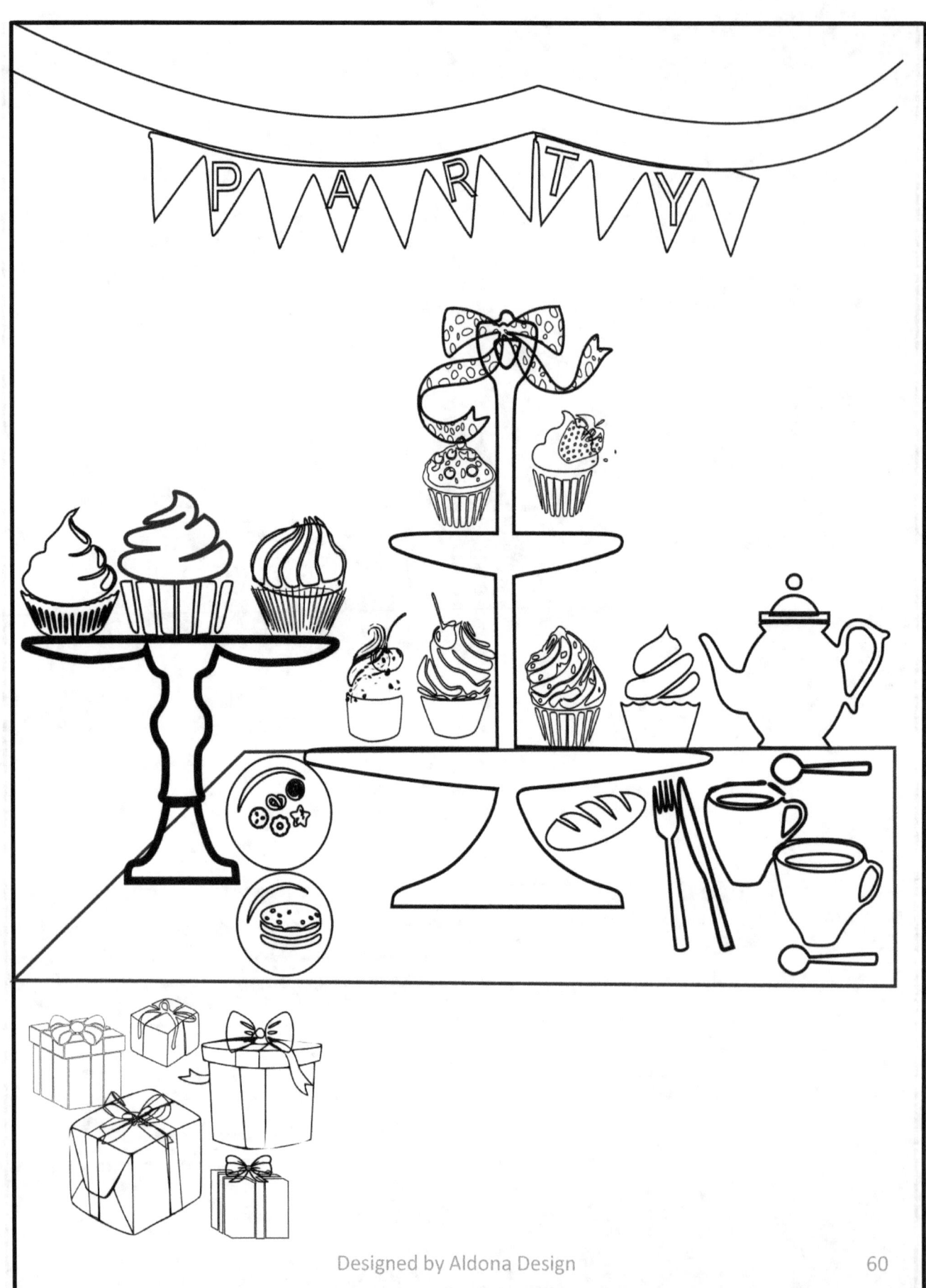

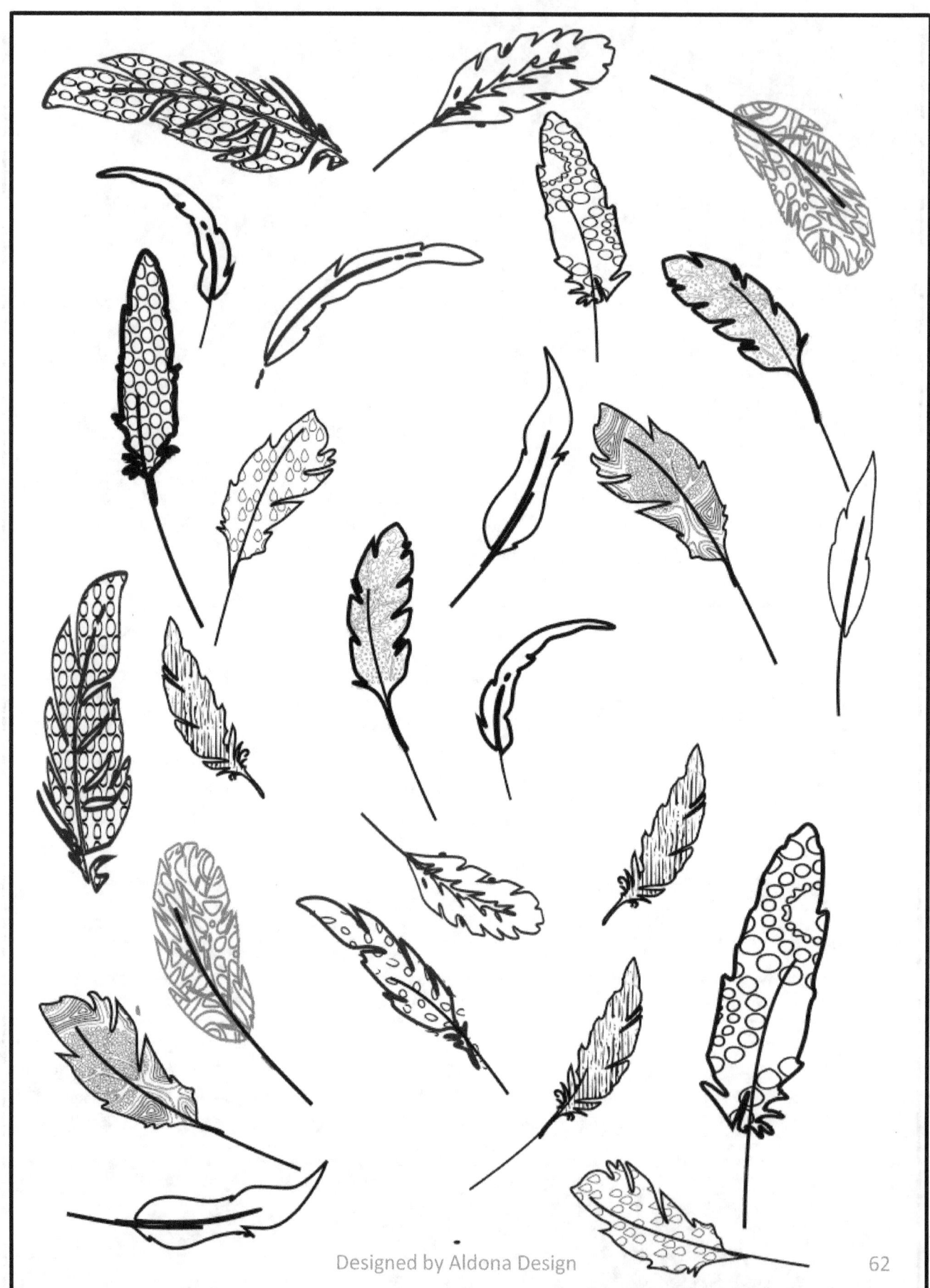

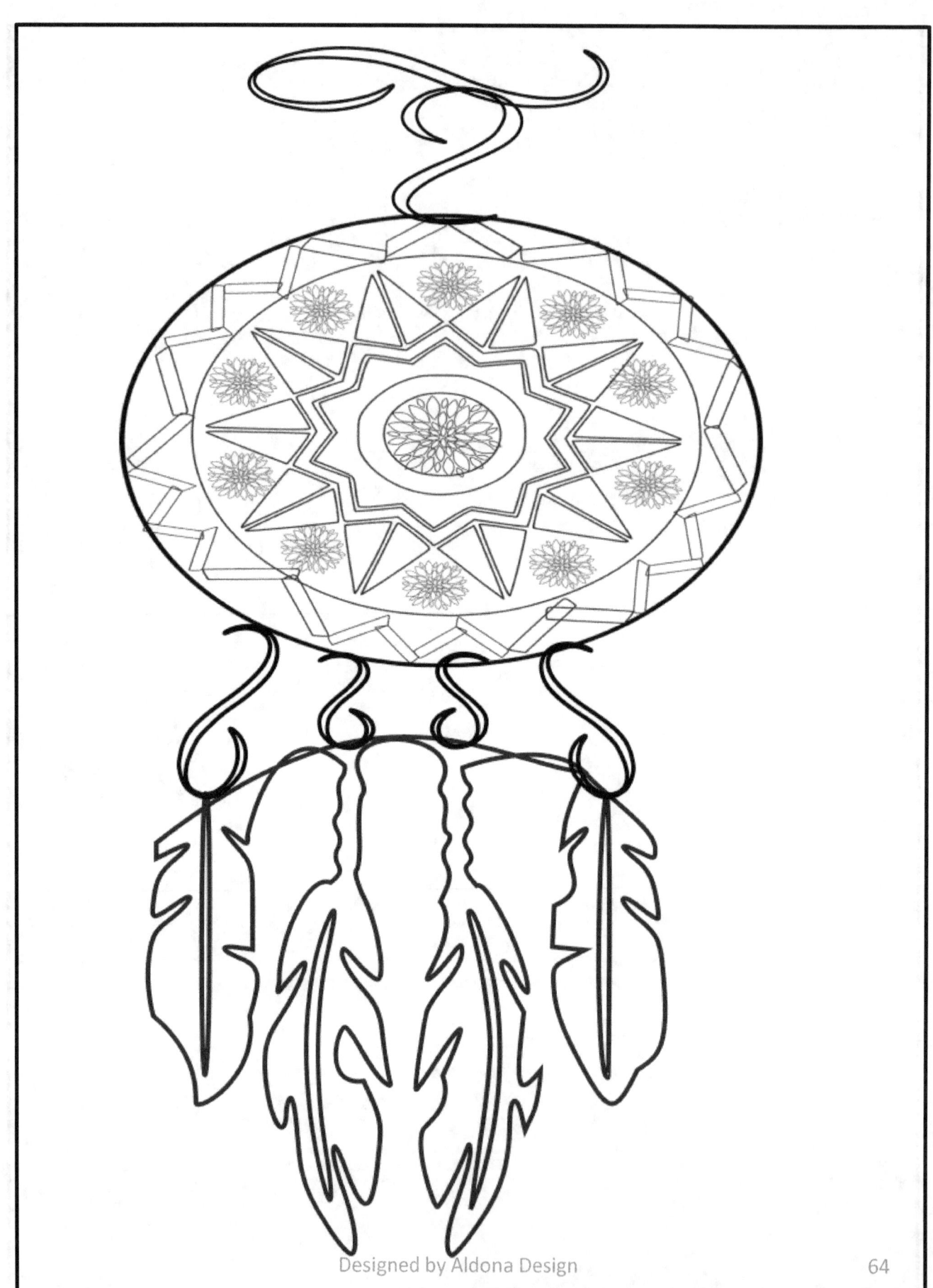

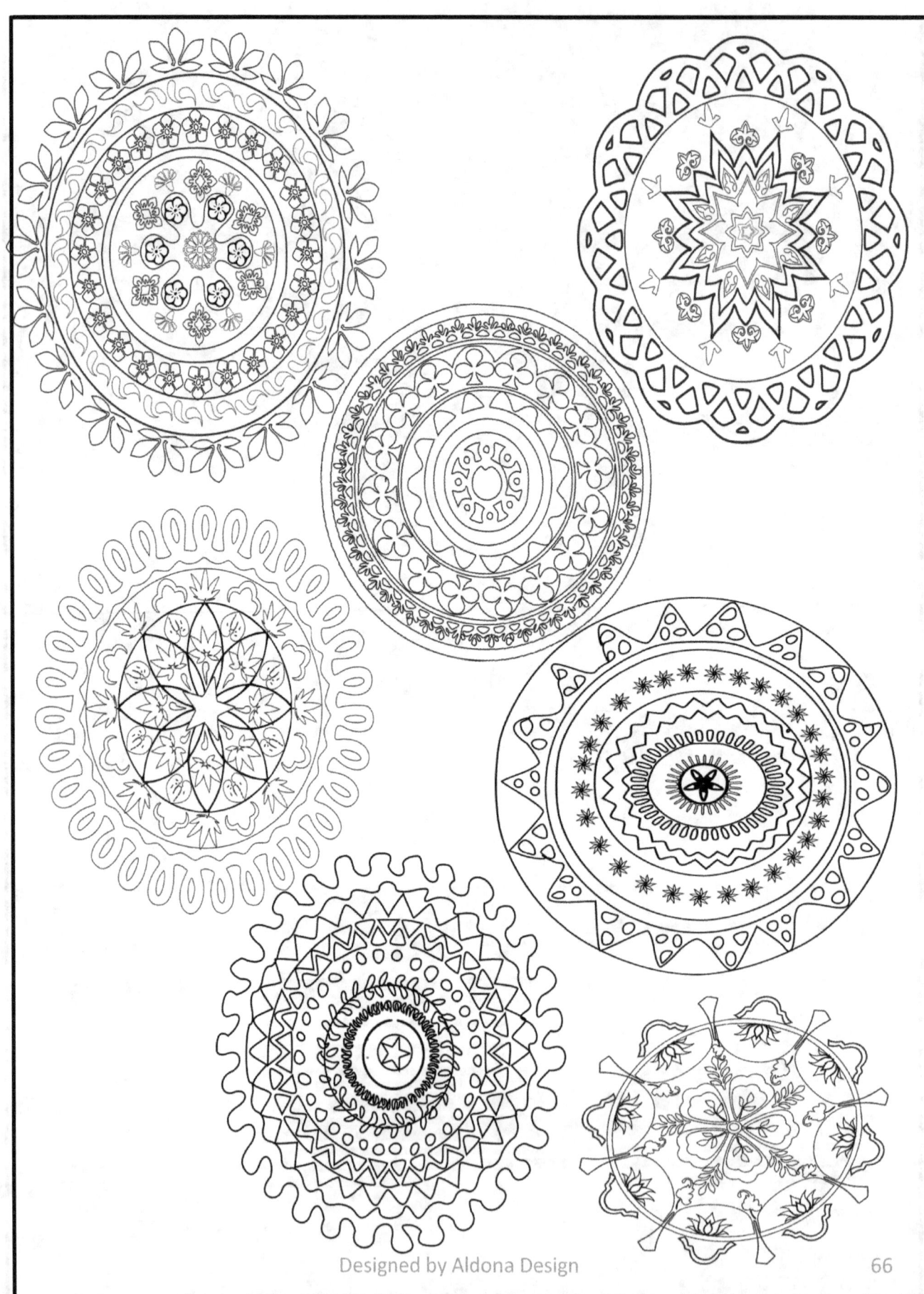

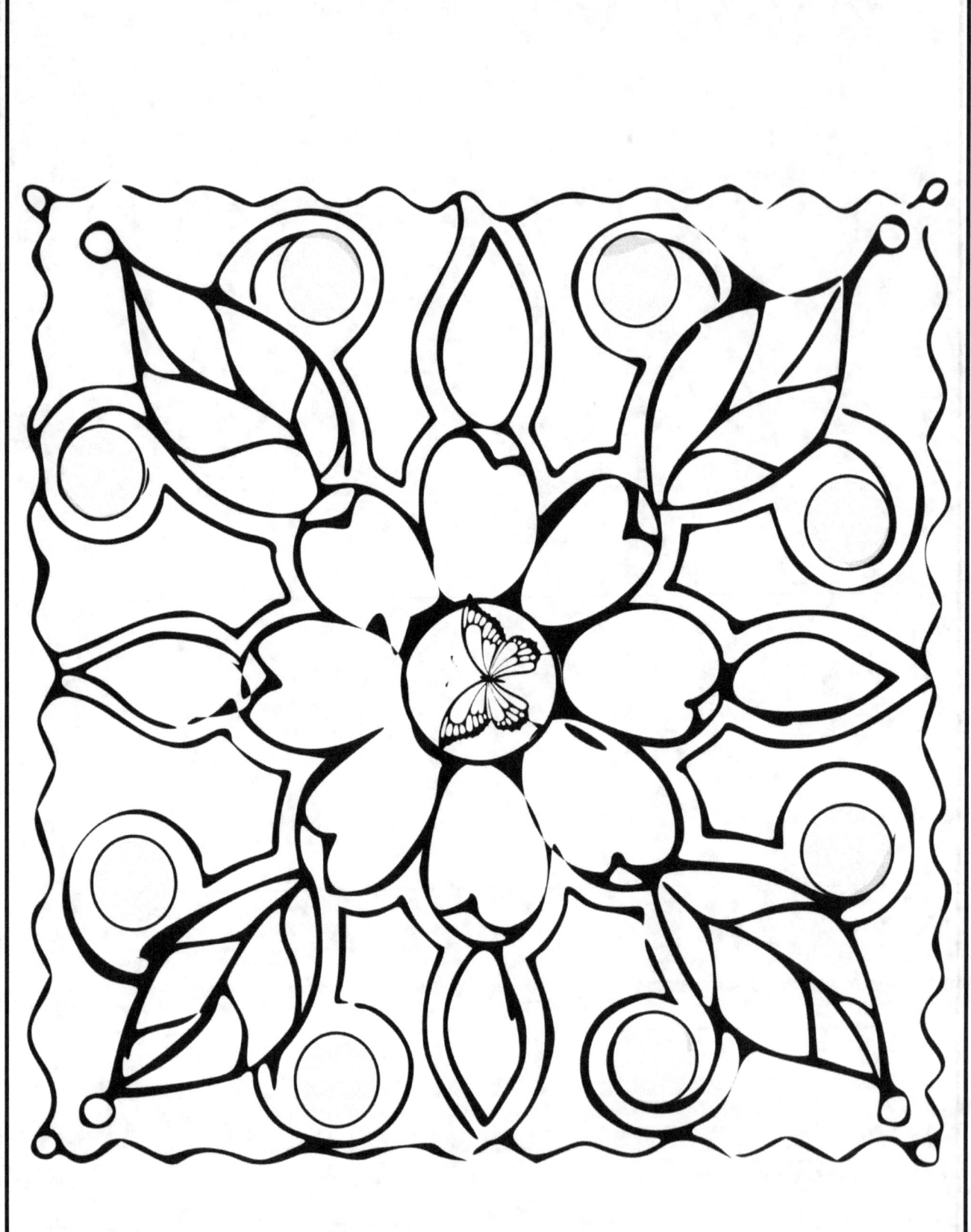

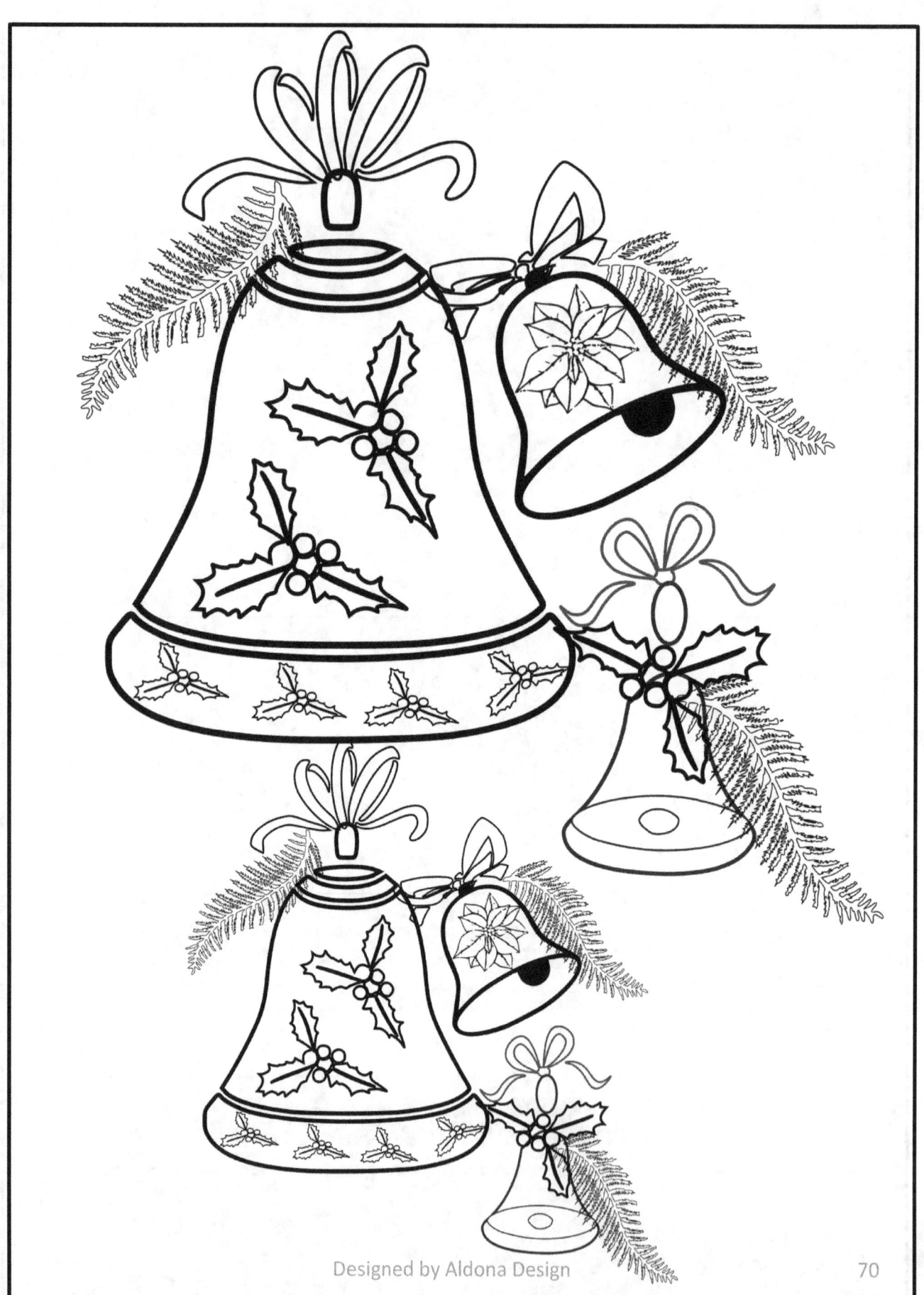

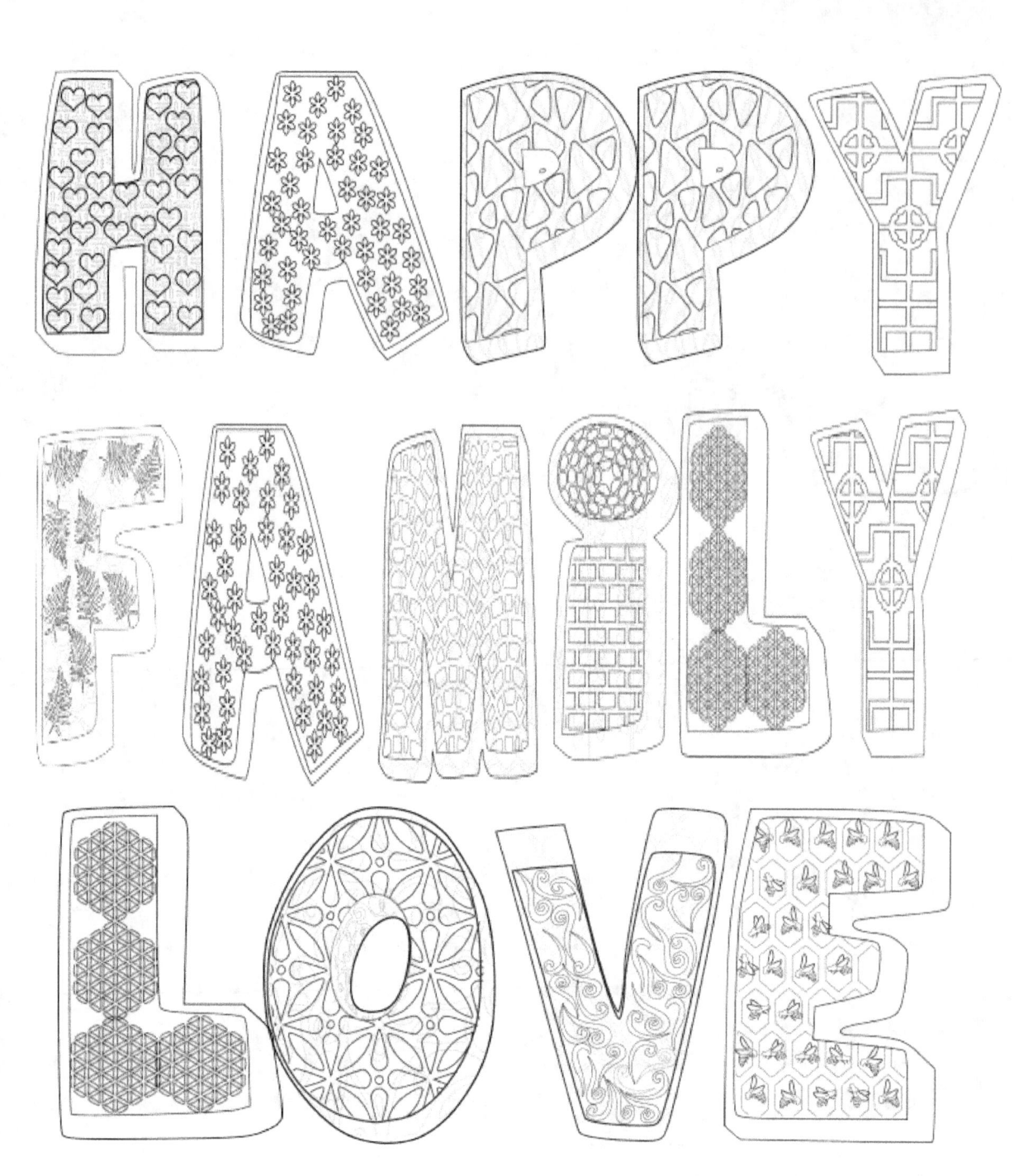

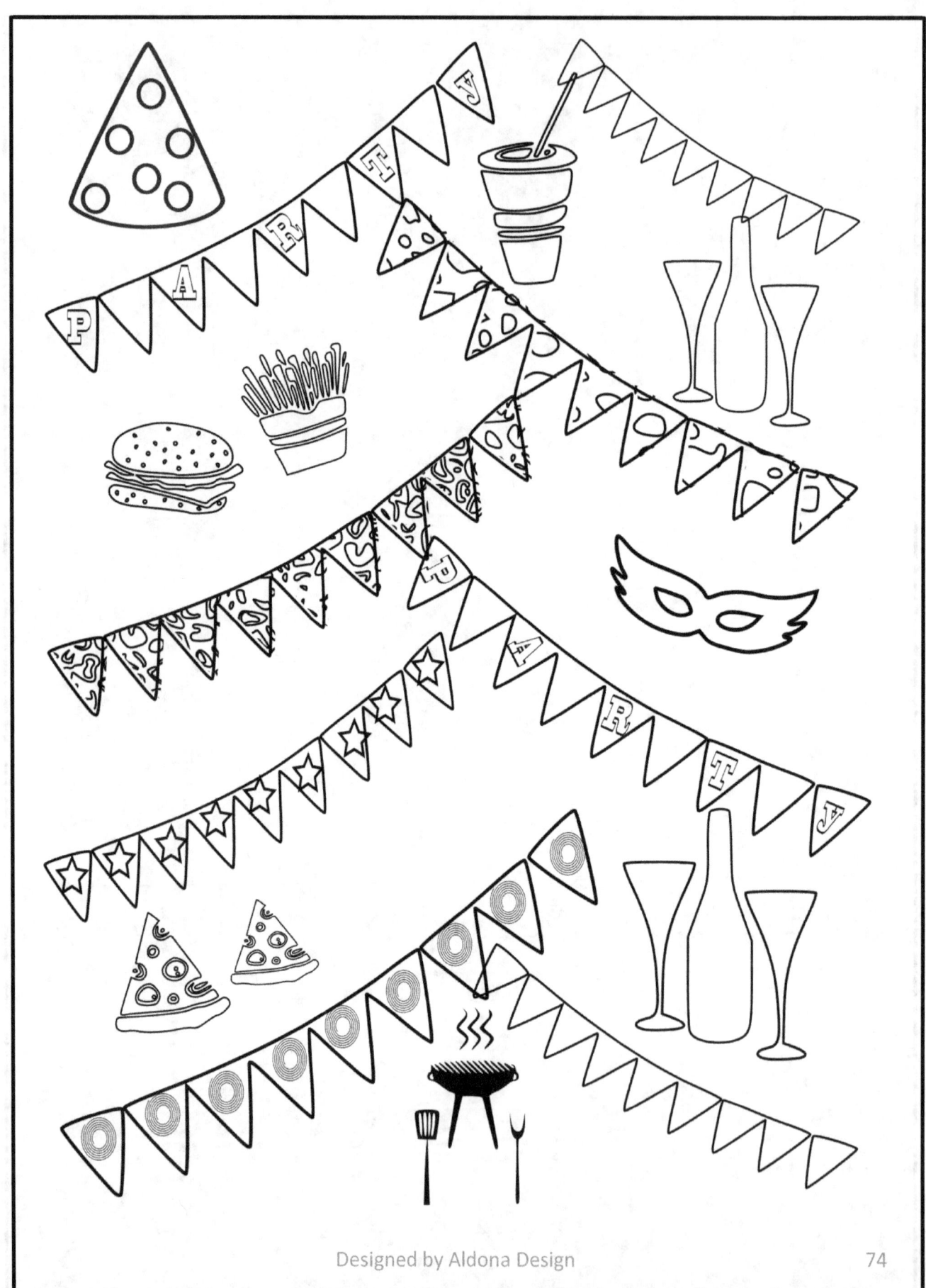

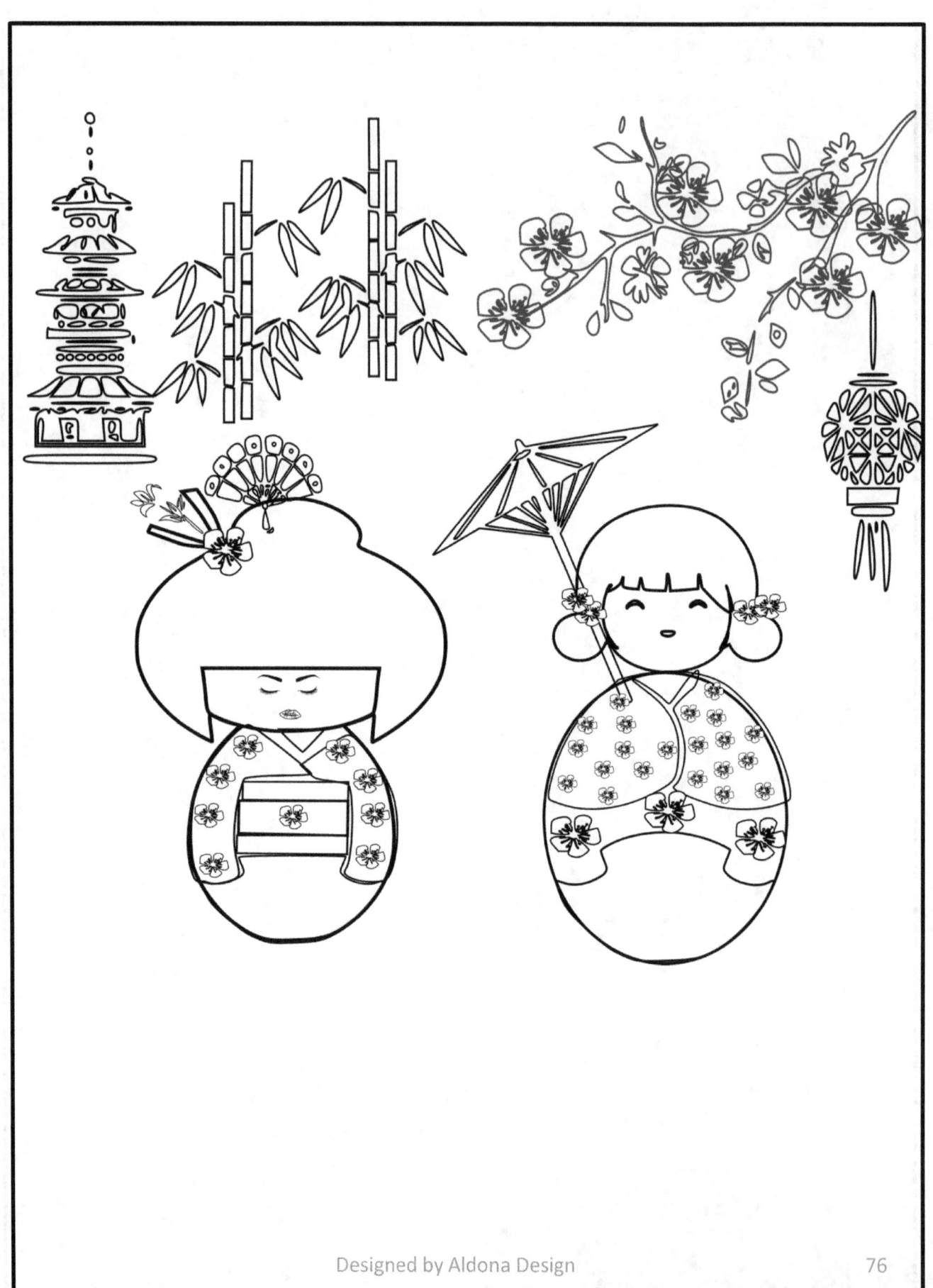

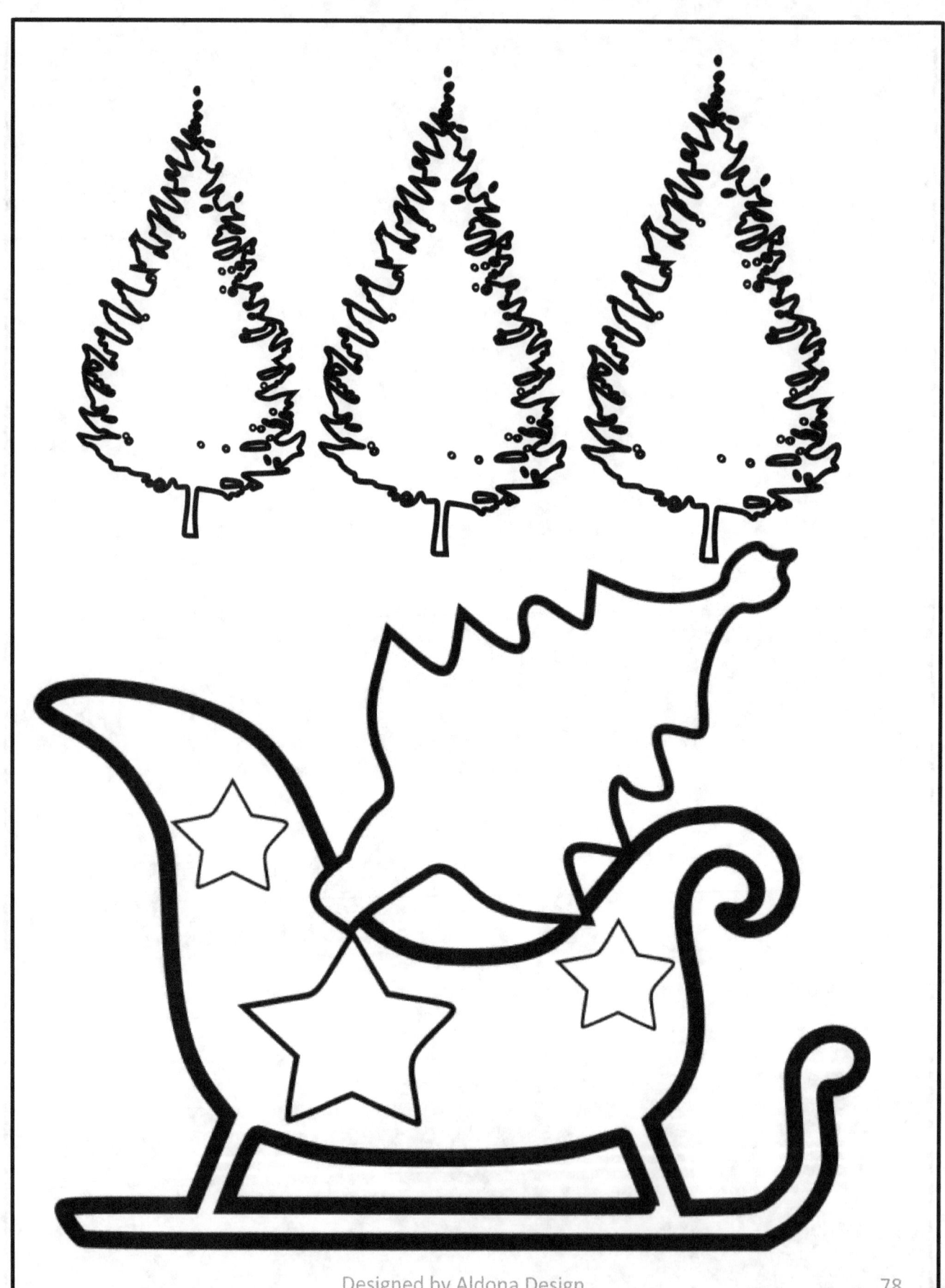

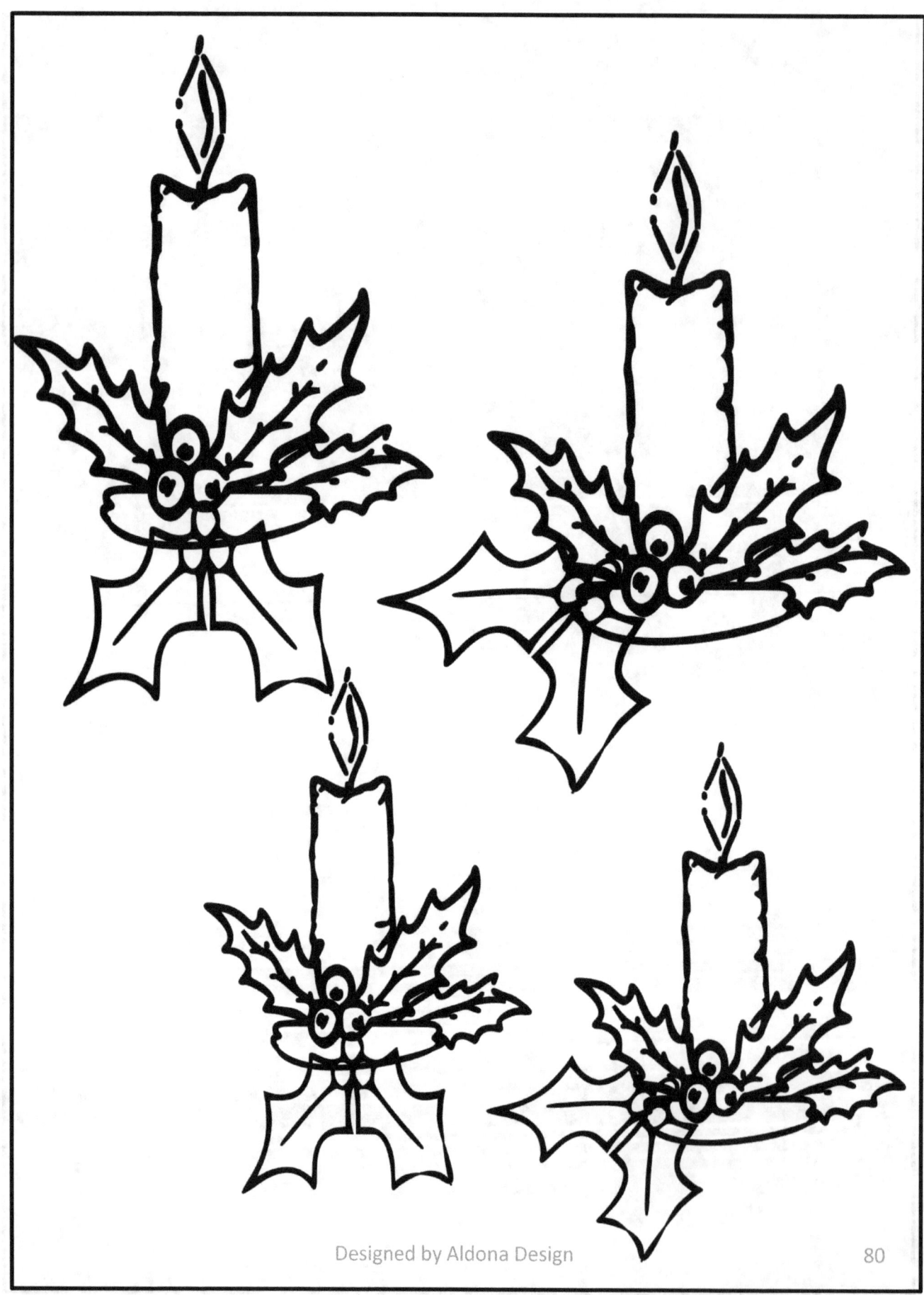

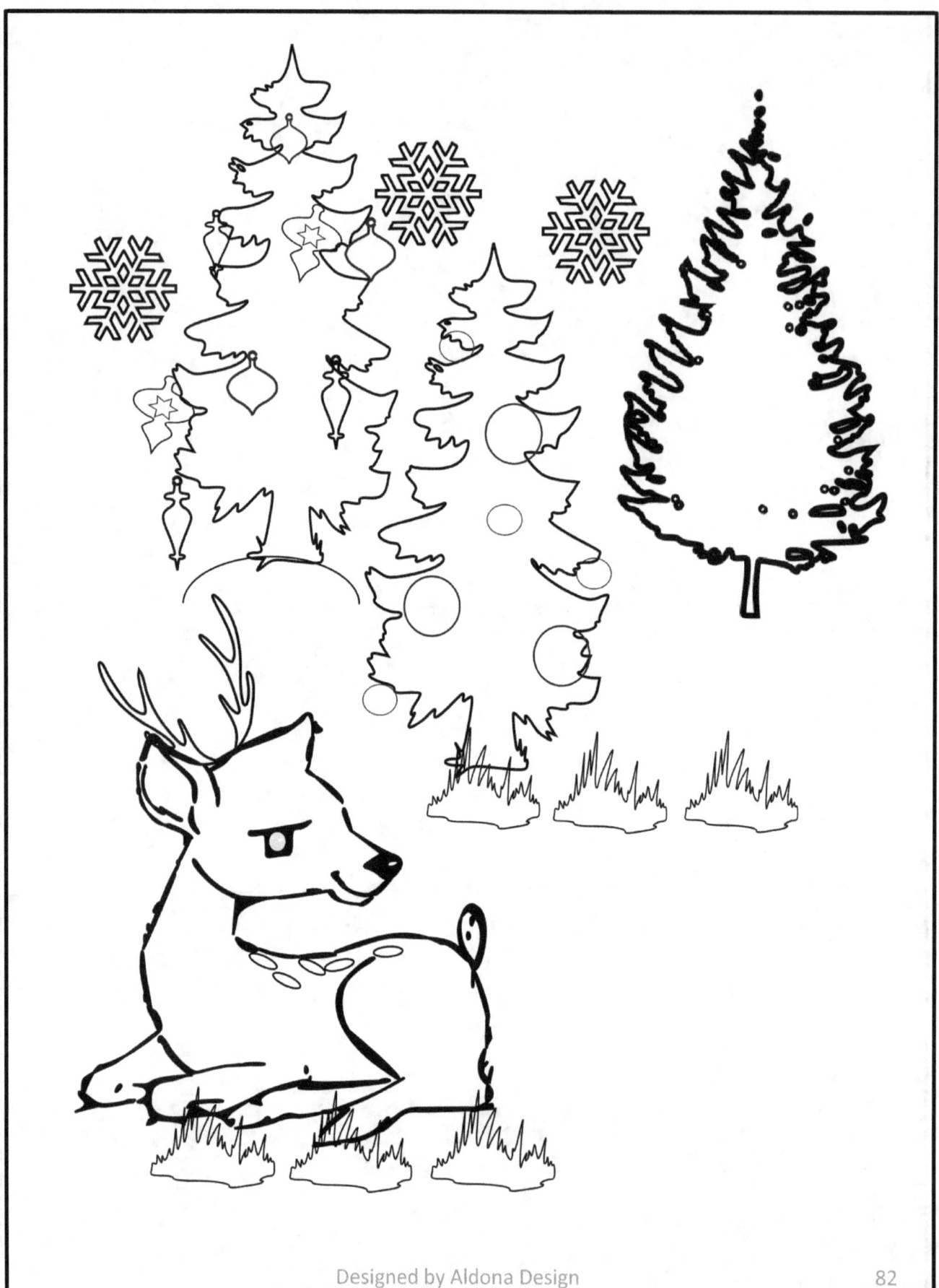

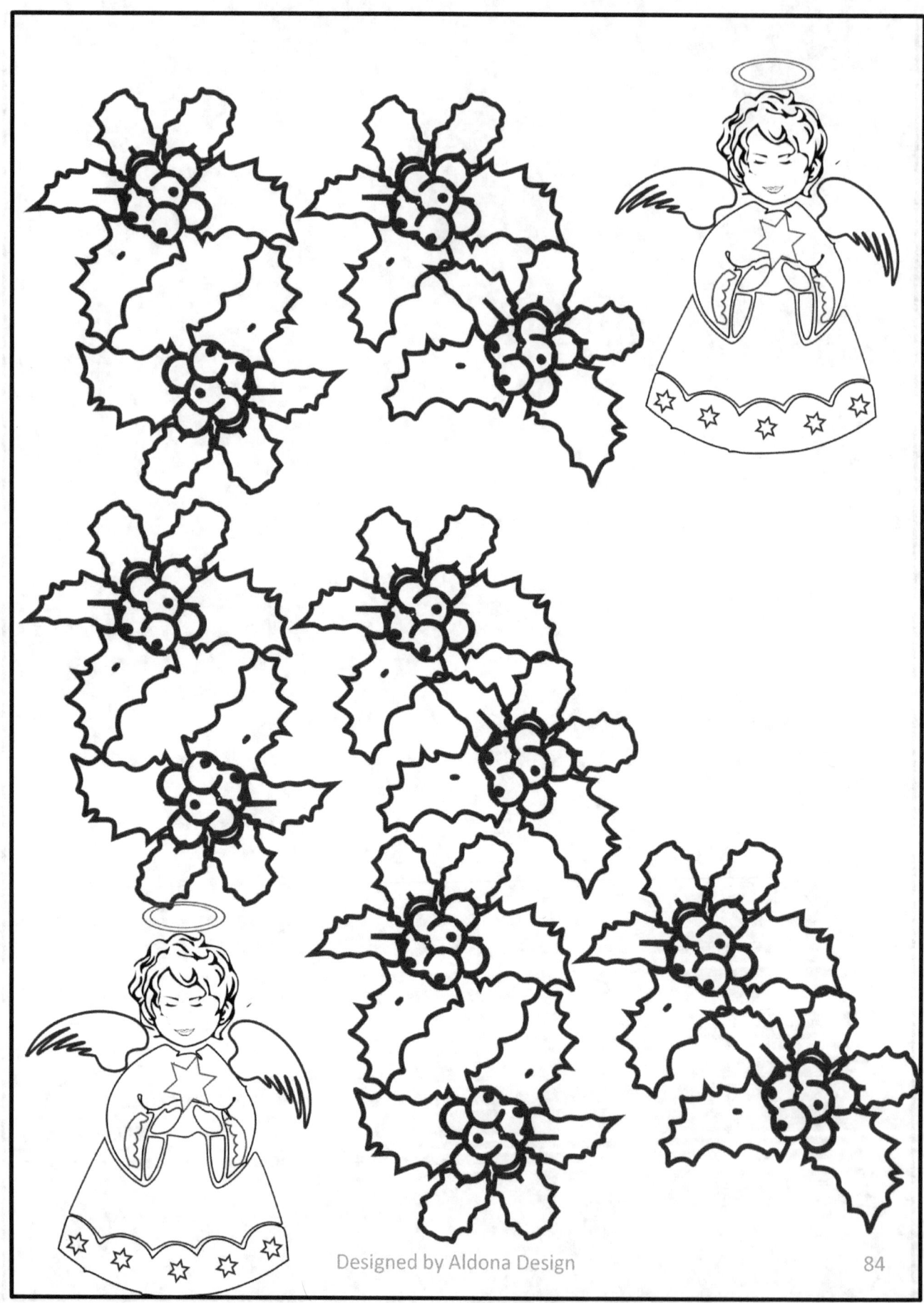

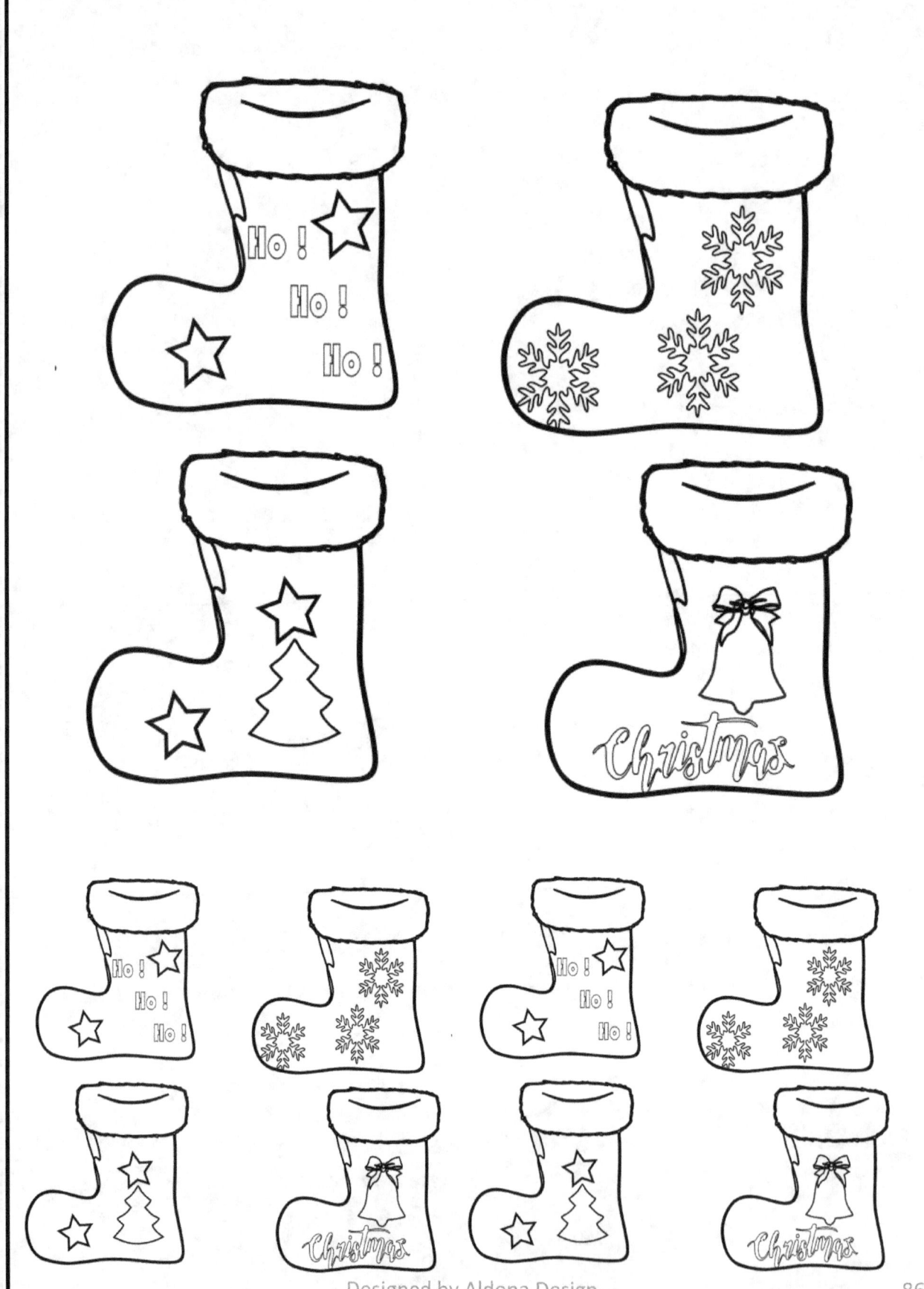

MERRY CHRISTMAS

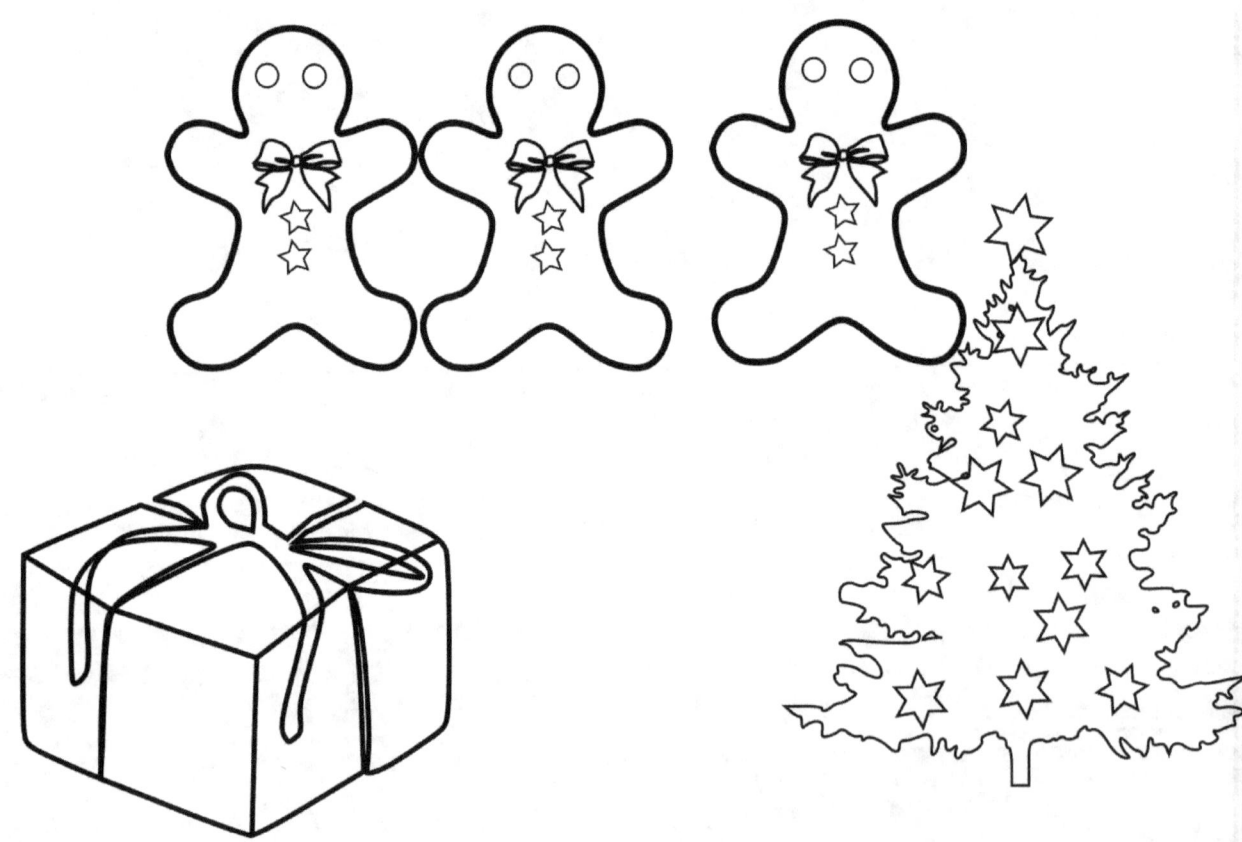

Ornaments

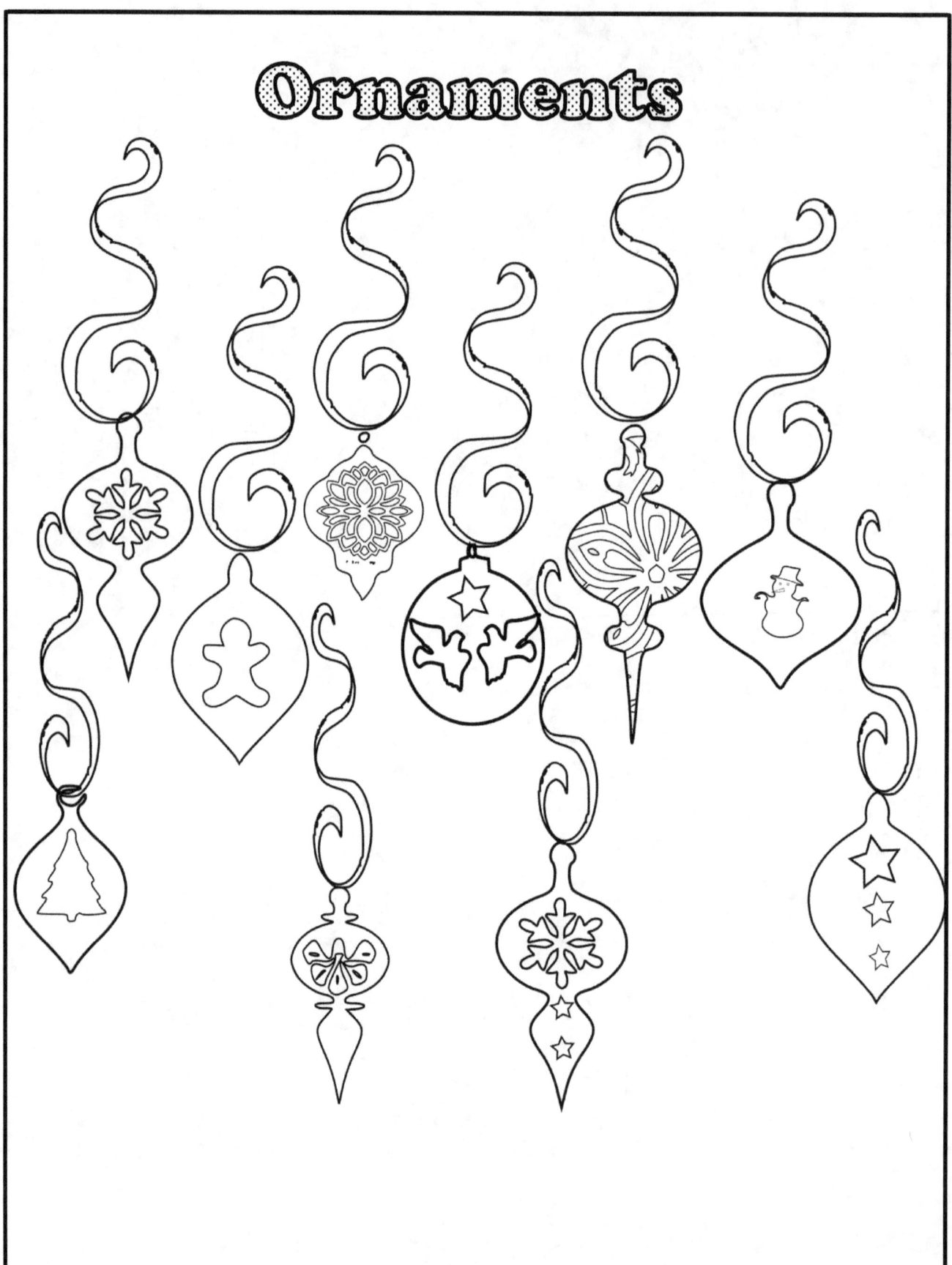

Wreaths

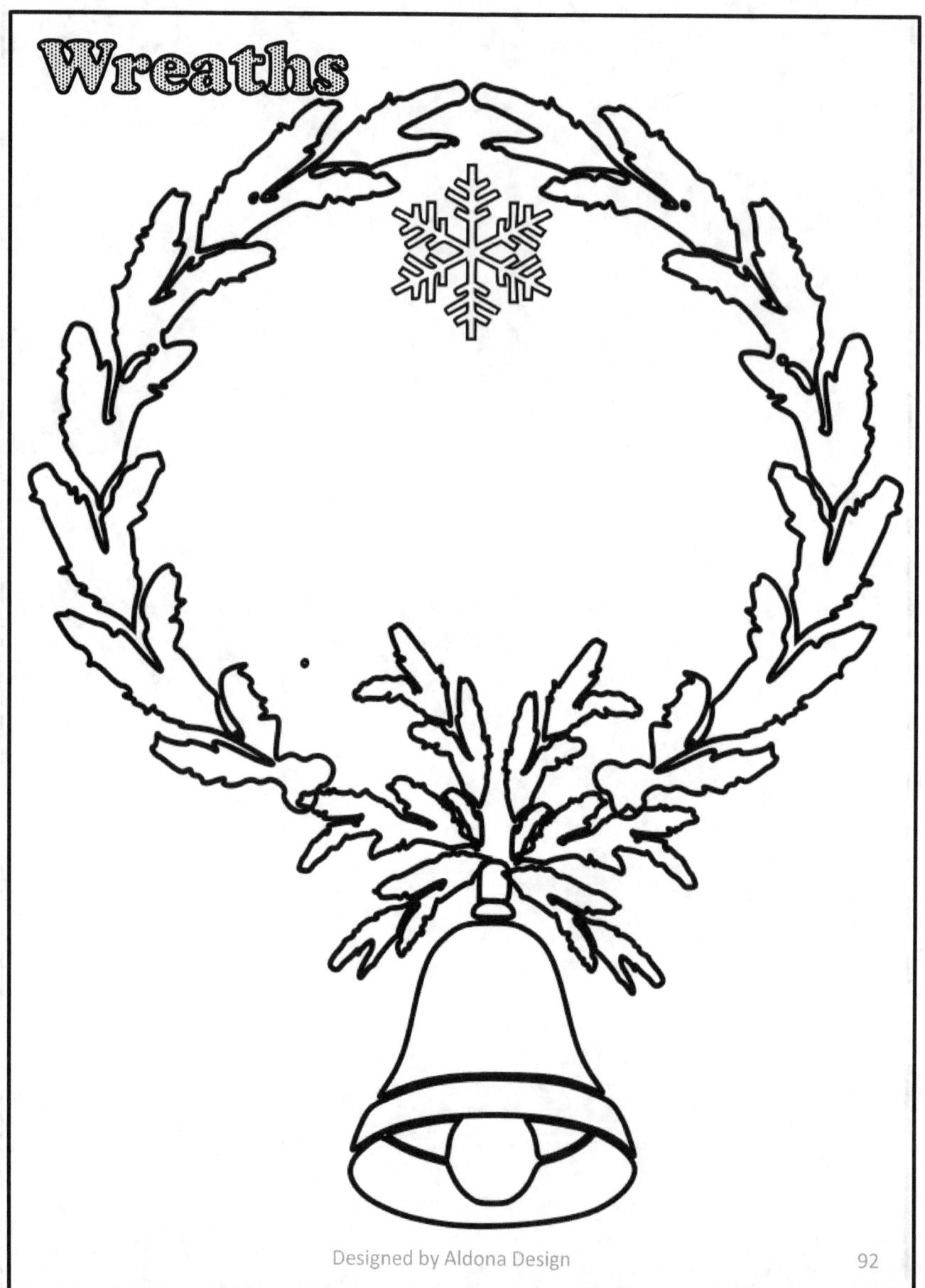

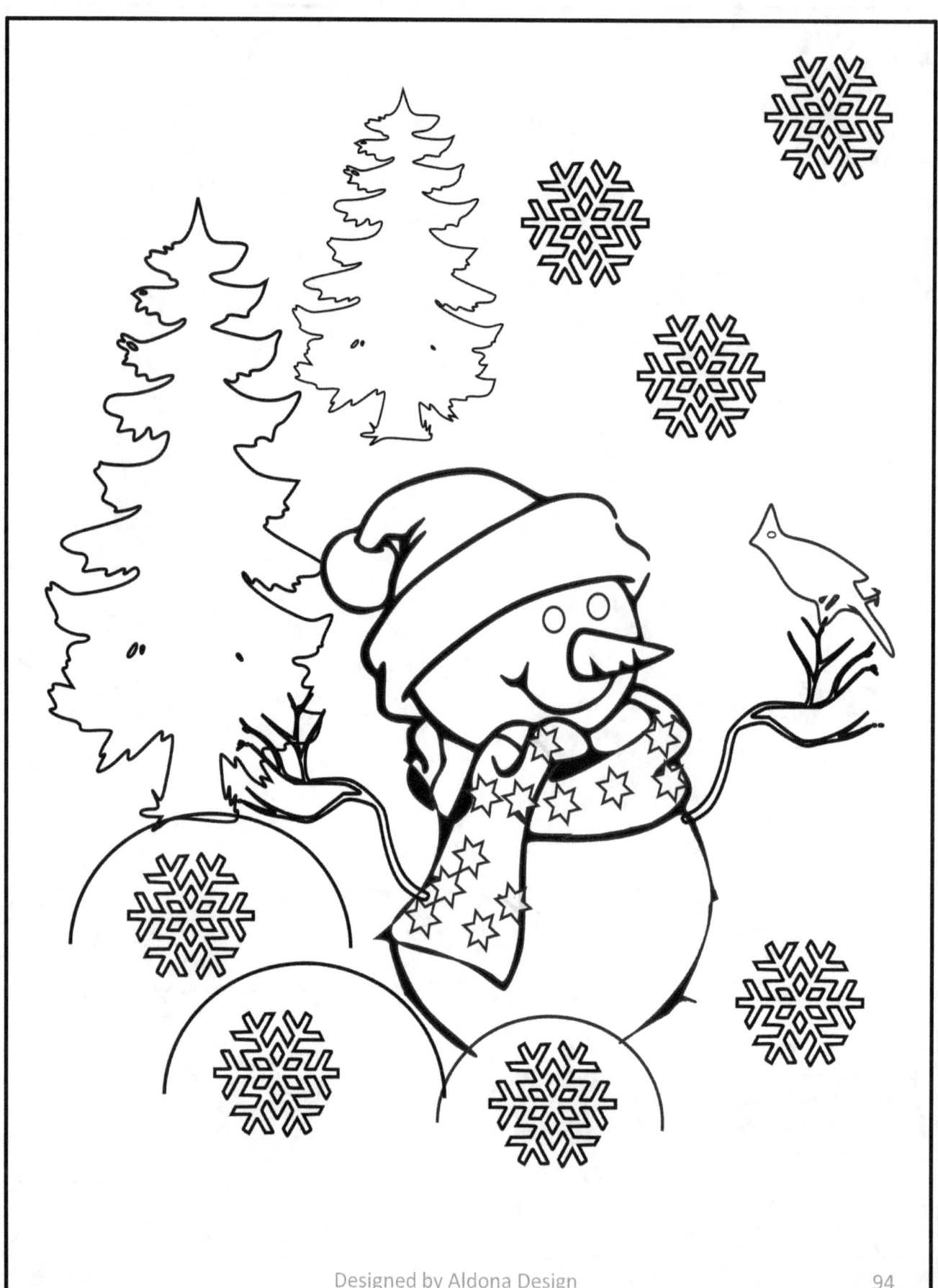

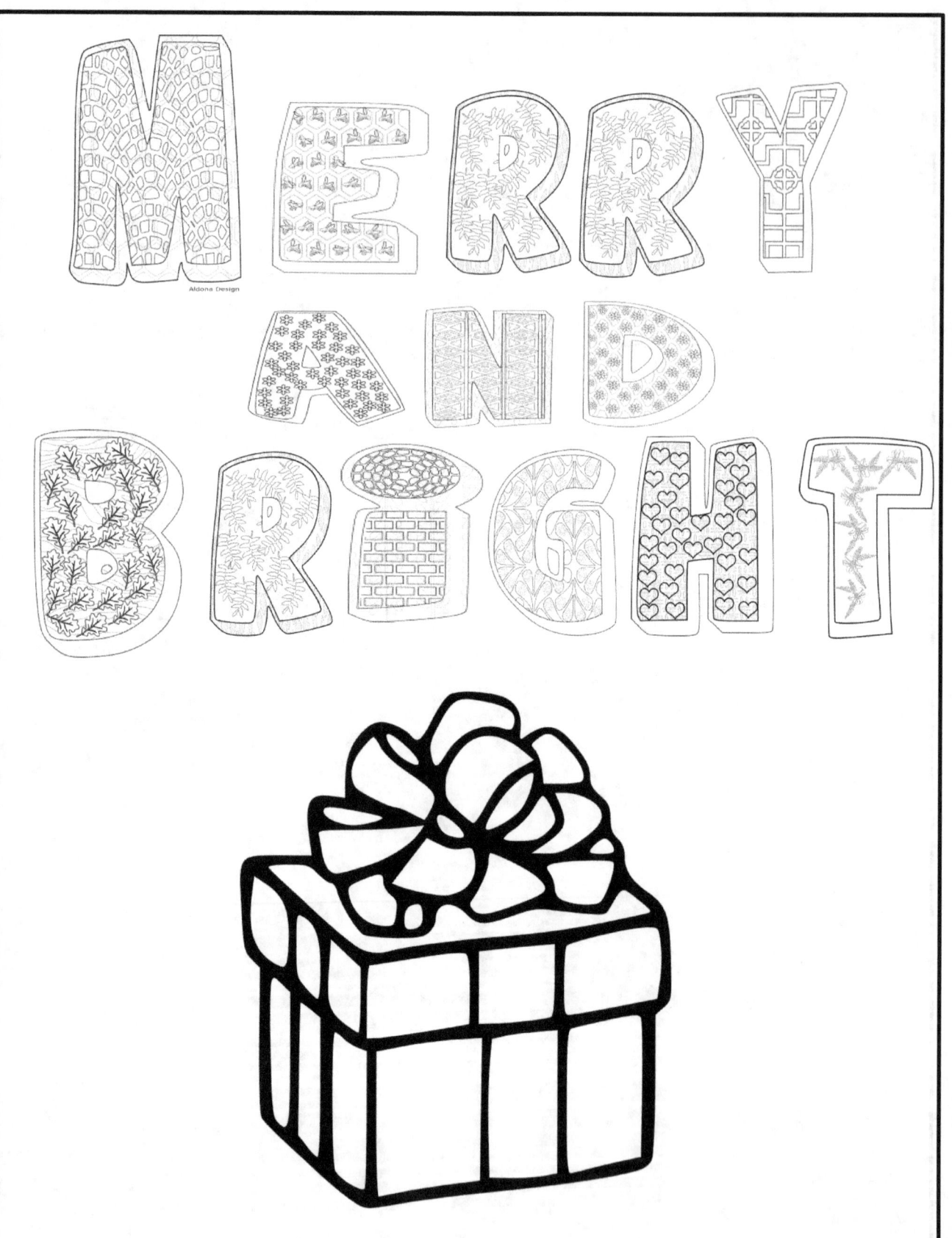

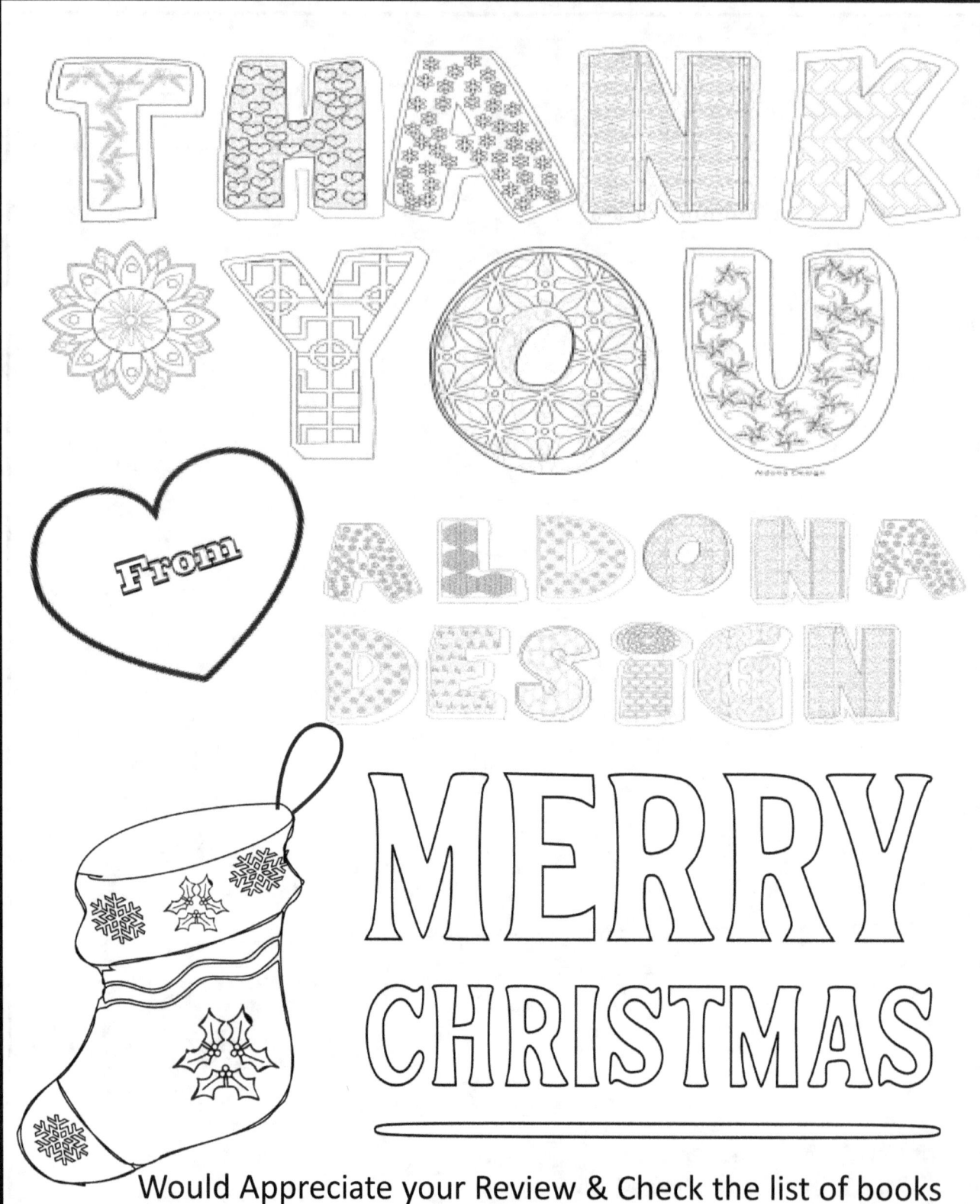

THANK YOU

From

ALDONA DESIGN

MERRY CHRISTMAS

Would Appreciate your Review & Check the list of books
On our Author Central Page (Link Below)
https://www.amazon.com/Aldona-Design

THANK YOU

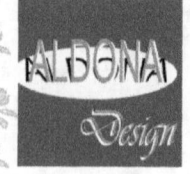

List of other book Title /Number by Aldona Design

- Therapeutic Colouring book: 1097666700
- Christmas Colouring Book For Kids: 1081432489
- Therapeutic Colouring Book III: 1687402108
- Therapeutic Coloring book IV: 1693086476
- Gift tags: 1690654244
- Monochrome Scrapbooking paper & design Elements (20 pages for Craft Projects) 109850335X
- Daily Gratitude Journal: 1691326143
- Character Sketch Book: 1691097772
- Landscape Sketch Book: 1695920074
- My Music notebook (120 pages) 1096141590
- Busy Mothers 1096908638
- For Dads (Planner for Dads) 1099823951
- For Dentist (Planner for a Dentist) 1070203378
- Hair stylist (Planner) 1078240760
- The Special Bride to be (Planner) 1079392483
- Recipe Notebook (to write your Recipes) 1080650474
- Weekly Meal Plan (Notebook to Plan Meals) 108065691X
- Wine Tasting Log Book: 169369400X
- Calendar Journal: 169259981X
- My Own Nail Art Design: 1686035950
- Type the number to the end of the link to view the above Titles, More books in store

https://www.amazon.com/gp/product/

www.ingramcontent.com/pod-product-compliance
Lightning Source LLC
Chambersburg PA
CBHW081010170526
45158CB00010B/2992